# FEELINGS ARE REAL
# Group Activities
# for Children

## Leader Manual

**Kristi Lane, Ph.D.**
Winona State University
Psychology Department
Minne Hall
Winona, Minnesota 55987

**Accelerated Development Inc.**
Publishers
Muncie, Indiana

# FEELINGS ARE REAL
## Group Activities for Children
## LEADER MANUAL

Technical Development:    Virginia Cooper
                          Tanya Dalton
                          Marguerite Mader
                          Sheila Sheward

Graphic art supplied by Dynamic Graphics Inc.
                        6000 N. Forrest Park Drive
                        Peoria, IL 61614-3592

ISBN: 1-55959-014-9

**ACCELERATED DEVELOPMENT INC., PUBLISHERS**
3400 Kilgore Avenue, Muncie, IN 47304-4896
Toll Free Order Number 1-800-222-1166

# ACKNOWLEDGEMENTS

This project began in the mid-1980s. Along the way many people assisted in completing various tasks. Manuscript preparation was executed by Karen Edwards and Robin Pruka. Lisa Loomis provided skillful editorial assistance. Terry Schwarze gave advice about the use of design in the preparation of worksheets. Winona State University provided assistance to pilot the group formats used in this manual. Dynamic Graphics, Inc., 6000 N. Forest Park Drive, Peoria, IL, 61614-3592, allowed Clipper Art to be used in the preparation of the workbooks. I appreciate the valuable assistance of all these individuals. Finally, I thank all of the children who have participated in this project and have taught me so much.

# FOREWORD

Teachers interact with children during a major developmental task of childhood—that of going to school. Teachers are important mentors and guides for the children in their classes. In most elementary school classes subject matter, such as social studies, science, reading, spelling, and others, are taught. In this "class" children are taught to identify, label, and understand their feelings. Each session presents a new concept and the opportunity to lead one or two activities in which children can participate. Children will complete workbook activities that are geared to their age. These activities are completed by working both in small groups and individually.

The end of each activity is designed to help you evaluate that activity. In this way, you can mold the *Feelings Are Real* activities to best suit you and your classroom. Intermediate age children record their feelings at the end of each exercise. The leader's role is to make comments to each student. In this way, the student gets personal encouragement.

# TABLE OF CONTENTS

**ACKNOWLEDGEMENTS** ..................................................... **iii**

**FOREWORD** ............................................................. **v**

**PART I  RATIONALE AND ORIENTATION** ........................... **1**

*Feelings are Real: Group Activities for Children* ........................ 3
    *Rationale* .............................................................. 3
        *Why Intervene?* .............................................. 4
        *Why Group?* ................................................. 5
    *Theoretical Orientation* .............................................. 6
        *Research Base* ............................................... 7
        *Rational Emotive Therapy (RET)* ............................. 7
        *Cognitive Behavioral Therapy (CBT)* ......................... 7
    *Summary* ............................................................. 9

**PART II  STRUCTURE AND ORGANIZATION** ..................... **11**

*Group Essentials* ........................................................ 13
        *Background* ................................................. 13
        *Mechanics of Beginning* ..................................... 13
        *Group Facilitator* ........................................... 13
        *Size* ....................................................... 14
        *Session Topics* .............................................. 14
        *Termination* ................................................ 14
    *Stages of Group Development* ........................................ 15
        *Security Stage* .............................................. 15
        *Acceptance Stage* ........................................... 17
        *Responsibility Stage* ........................................ 18
        *Work Stage* ................................................ 19
        *Closing Stage/Termination Stage* ........................... 19
    *Basic Skills for Group Leaders* ...................................... 20
        *Listening* .................................................. 20
        *Reflecting* ................................................. 20
        *Encouraging* ............................................... 21
        *Open-ended Questions* ...................................... 22

    *Focusing* .......................................................... *22*
    *Summary of Skills* ........................................... *23*
  *Forming Groups* .............................................. *23*
    *Starting a Group* ............................................. *23*
    *Understanding Sources of Support* ............... *23*
    *Guidelines for the Proposal* ......................... *25*
    *Commitment to Be a Group Leader* ............. *25*
    *Classroom Groups* ......................................... *26*
  *Leader Outcomes* ............................................ *27*

## PART III MANUAL FOR PRIMARY WORKBOOK
## GRADES 2 AND 3 ............................................. **29**

*Manual for Primary Workbook* ............................. *31*
  *Introduction* ...................................................... *31*
  *Group Sessions* ................................................ *32*
  *Session 1 Introduction* .................................... *35*
  *Session 2 Rules, Rules* .................................... *39*
  *Session 3 Sharing Feelings* ............................. *42*
  *Session 4 Happy and Sad* ................................ *49*
  *Session 5 Afraid and Worried* .......................... *55*
  *Session 6 Anger* .............................................. *60*
  *Session 7 Stress* .............................................. *66*
  *Session 8 Relaxation* ........................................ *69*
  *Session 9 Friendship* ........................................ *74*
  *Session 10 Self-Concept* .................................. *80*

## PART IV MANUAL FOR INTERMEDIATE WORKBOOK
## GRADES 4, 5, AND 6 ...................................... **87**

*Manual for Intermediate Workbook* ...................... *89*
  *Introduction* ...................................................... *89*
  *Group Sessions* ................................................ *90*
  *Session 1 Getting to Know You* ........................ *93*
  *Session 2 Sharing* ............................................ *96*
  *Session 3 Feelings* ............................................ *99*
  *Session 4 Assertive Behavior* ........................... *103*
  *Session 5 Aggressive and Nonassertive Behaviors* ........ *108*
  *Session 6 Anger* .............................................. *115*
  *Session 7 My Strengths* .................................... *120*
  *Session 8 Decision Making* ............................... *125*
  *Session 9 Relationships—Family* ...................... *128*
  *Session 10 Friendship* ...................................... *131*

## BIBLIOGRAPHY ............................................. **135**

## INDEX ........................................................... **139**

## ABOUT THE AUTHOR ................................. **147**

# LIST OF FIGURES

1   Multiple layer concept within a school .......................... 24

2   Topics and activities for primary school level children
listed by sessions ......................................................... 33

3   Topics and activities for intermediate school
level children listed by session ...................................... 91

# Part I

# RATIONALE
# and
# ORIENTATION

# Feelings Are Real
# Group Activities
# for Children

Group support is especially important for children and youth. This is evidenced in their natural affiliations with peers and with family. Both of these groups can either facilitate or reduce the youth's prosocial behavior. A positive impact can be made on children and adolescents if the power of the peer group can be utilized to assist children and adolescents while they develop their identity, self-esteem, emotional assertiveness, and coping skills. Intensive group work will be effective in helping school-age youth develop their ability to adapt to the world. Further, each child's competence will be strengthened by involving the major components of the child's world: the school, the home, and the community. Therefore, school-age children who experience emotional, social, and family difficulties will be the target population for this intervention project which will focus on group procedures as the primary method of developing healthy, adaptive behaviors.

## RATIONALE

Winning in the world can be equated with succeeding by adapting. The child who is winning will tend to show certain characteristics. The child will have social skills appropriate to the age level, such as relating to peers and feeling at ease. A sense of competence or ability to master stressful situations will be demonstrated by the child. Therefore, the child who sees a problem as a challenge instead of an insurmountable barrier is displaying competence and self-confidence. Additionally, the child's willingness to utilize adults as resources or teachers is showing a sign of winning as well as developing a sense of independence, defined as being capable of making decisions based on internal reasons not on external influences. Finally, the winning child is achieving and receiving recognition from family, school, and friends which can include hobbies, school, and activities. The child needs to feel the sense of mastery while developing skills which are recognized by others. The winning child is meeting challenges, using skills, developing new skills, reaching out to adults and peers, and developing an inner sense of character.

**Why Intervene?**

The decade of the 80s witnessed the change of and perhaps the undermining of the natural support systems of the child. Family roles and relations have changed and have resulted in increasing fragmentation in the lives of families. This is evident in the increasing number of single-parent homes, the shortage of adequate child care, the number of children who "mind the house" until one or both of their parents return home from work late in the evening. For the child, the result may be an increasing sense of impermanence in daily life: some call this ever-changing routine *stress.*

School adds to the demands of the child's world. The education system is being criticized for falling short of goals of education. In turn, the school pushes the child to prove that a certain quantity of knowledge is attained. School, the major developmental task of childhood, becomes a source of frustration, demand, and stress. The media makes clear computer skills are a prerequisite for success at school. Thus, the child is in the center of two crucial systems both producing stress, turmoil, and demands without providing challenge or safety.

The peer group is subjected to a "pseudosophistication" from the media. For example, the speeding up of the child's development is seen when a twelve-year-olds fashionable dress is to appear eighteen-years old. Many of the privileges formally reserved for the teen years have become boring for even the preteen. Perhaps, this is because the child's knowledge about the world has increased due to the media and the pervasive attitude that children can understand whatever an adult can: in reality *children are more similar to adults in their feelings than in their understanding.* This can make much of the child's knowledge about the world incomprehensible to the child at a level of deep understanding. This partition between actions and understanding is confusing and contributes to stress for the child.

Family, school, and friends—all natural support system— have been rendered less effective during this last decade. The child experiences a fast-paced, ever-changing world in which reactions are expected and given quickly. The child/ adolescent appears grown-up because they have copied ways of dealing with the world from media, teachers, friends, and parents. The future of these natural supports can be in the lack of time and/or encouragement given to the child to construct actively an individual realty. Group support can provide a place to learn about feelings.

## Why Group?

Children have needs for belonging, security, recognition, and affection. Interactions with other children can help to meet these needs through support, shared feelings, and ideas. As children in a group form trusting relationships with the group leader and members, they begin to feel more accepted by others and less alone in coping with their problems. Group problem solving teaches decision-making skills and provides models of new behaviors. In addition, the support of the group can take away feelings of isolation. The skills learned in a group apply to all human interactions. These skills are among the basic skills which people most possess: communication, identification of feelings, empathy with others, social skills, definition of goals, and self-esteem.

Yalom (1975) believed that nine factors operate in a group and contribute to its effectiveness. He believed group cohesiveness, defined as feelings of belonging and acceptance, solidarity and loyalty, support, and caring, helps make a group cohesive. The more cohesive a group is, the more valuable the group becomes. In a group, persons act the way they do in real life. This dimension of a group is called interpersonal learning and allows that the group can play a pivotal role in attempts to change. Another function of a group is advice/guidance/information. Initially, the group leader, or facilitator, is primarily responsible for this function. Later, the group members become altruistic in giving mutual help and support. In addition, a person can learn by identification/imitation/modeling. The group member can learn from the facilitator, the other group members, and norms or rules of the group. Yalom also believed that groups have universal qualities and offer hope to their members. The structure of a group can allow some members to re-enact family relationships. For example, if certain members viewed the leader as the authority then those members may react to that person like they reacted to their mother/father. Finally, group provides the catharsis, or a venting of one's emotions. In a group setting, catharsis can be safe and channeled into appropriate expression of feelings.

## THEORETICAL ORIENTATION

**The primary objective of this manual is to help group leaders teach children how to identify, label, understand, and cope with their feelings.** Essentially, the feelings level, or heart, interacts with the cognitive level, or mind, through the behavior, or actions. *So, heart talks to mind through our actions.* This means we can simultaneously possess different levels of understanding. That is, we can cognitively understand and be able to explain an event. If our understanding stops at the cognitive level some psychologists consider that the defense mechanism of intellectualization is being utilized. The problem with intellectualization is that we may not be able to truly understand our feelings or to cope with our feelings. At other times we may experience a feeling that is strong and heart-felt. Some people refer to this as a gut-level feeling. At the same time, we may have little or no understanding or explanation of our feelings. Some theoretical orientations refer to this as intuitive, meaning felt or sensed without the use of logical process or reasoning. The link between our mind and heart is our actions. In some ways, we watch our behaviors and feel their consequences. During this process our feelings and our thoughts begin to connect.

## Research Base

The theoretical orientation just described is eclectic but it mainly draws ideas from *Rational Emotive Therapy* (RET) and *cognitive behavioral therapy* (CBT). I will describe briefly each of these theories. Each theory has an extensive literature in texts, scientific research, and popular psychology books. Leaders who want more information on a given topic will not have problems finding it.

### Rational Emotive Therapy (RET)

Albert Ellis (Dryden & Ellis, 1988) is the major theoretician associated with RET. "The focus is on working with *thinking* and *acting* rather than primarily with expressing feelings. Therapy is seen as an *educational* process . . . teaching strategies for straight thinking" (Corey, 1986, p. 209). In RET our thoughts, emotions, and actions are viewed as being an interactive system. An emphasis is placed on rationality. People can develop irrational thoughts or beliefs. If this occurs, their emotions and actions become a response to their irrational beliefs. The key to changing behaviors is to change faulty beliefs. The change period is assisted by a therapist who accepts the client, listens to the clients, and helps to identify irrational beliefs. *Homework* and *bibliotherapy* are tools used to help the client change. The client is active and works on changing feelings and behavior. The therapist is directive and encourages the client to do new things and act in new ways. Through this active approach the client can utilize new learning. RET utilizes behavioral techniques of *rewards* and *penalties*. Negative emotions may be the result of irrational thinking which can be changed by challenging the irrational thoughts, replacing them with rational thoughts and then acting in a rational manner.

### Cognitive Behavioral Therapy (CBT)

Beck (1976) wrote that cognitive therapy "consists of all the approaches that alleviate psychological distress through the medium of correcting faulty conceptions and self-signals . . . We get to the person's emotions through his cognitions" (p. 24). In this approach, emphasis is placed on examining what the person cognitively tells the self while in a given situation. It is our cognitive interpretation of an event that causes our feelings. The therapist helps the client re-examine the situation for other alternative explanations of a situation.

A variation upon cognitive therapy is *cognitive behavioral therapy* (CBT). Again, the focus is that our cognitions mediate the world. When our behavior is maladaptive or our emotions negative, then CBT suggests examining our cognitions for possible sources of distortion. CBT with children concentrates on developing effective mediating strategies for the control of behavior. Meichenbaum (1977) discusses a three part process of change. First, the child learns self-observation. This includes listening to our cognitions and to what we tell ourselves (self-talk) about a situation. Second, the child learns to change the self-talk and to replace it with self-talk that is helpful in coping with a situation. Third, the child learns new behaviors for a situation. In CBT the therapist acts as an educator about cognitions and perceptions and as a model of new, coping behaviors.

Braswell and Kendall (1988) described a number of CBT interventions used with children. **Problem-solving training** is one technique these authors discuss. An early example of problem-solving is the "turtle" technique which was developed to help emotionally disturbed young children stop responding impulsively in social situations. Robin, Schneider, and Dolnick (1976) described their "turtle" technique as composed of 4 phases: (1) the "turtle" response consisting of lowering one's head and pulling in one's limbs as a response to threat, (2) relaxation training, (3) learning to find alternative solutions along with their consequences, and (4) social rewards for a child who uses the "turtle" response. Problem-solving can be used with families as well as with children.

A second CBT intervention is **verbal self-instructional training** defined by Braswell and Kendall (1988) as "self-directed statements of an internal dialogue that an individual uses to guide himself/herself through a problem-solving procedure" (p. 182). These authors described their method of teaching self-instruction as (1) clinician models self instruction, (2) child performs the task while clinician verbalizes self-instruction, (3) child solves problems while verbalizing self-instruction, and (4) child completes tasks using covert self-instruction. This self-instruction serves as a cognitive mediator of behavior. It also can be a source of feedback about performance. In self-instruction the child needs to learn the concepts behind self-talk and not merely to repeat memorized words. Children appear to best accomplish this goal by learning self-instruction utilizing a familiar task.

A third CBT intervention is **attribution retraining,** or the investigation of the children's causal explanation of behavior. Attributions of causality must be based in reality and be accurate if they can serve to guide the child's behavior in an adaptive way. Attribution retraining tries to get the "child to take more individual credit for his/her achievements, thus encouraging the child's experience in positive control and/or self-efficacy" (Braswell & Kendall, 1988, p. 191). At the same time some children find internal causes for situations or events truly outside themselves, such as a parent's divorce. The children who are internalizing the attribution will blame themselves for the divorce. In this case the clinician must help the child seek a realistic and external attribution of causality.

In CBT the clinician uses **modeling of behaviors.** The child learns by watching the adult perform, or model a behavior. The clinician also uses role-playing to teach social behaviors. Again, the learning is based upon experience gained through the role-play. The clinician uses traditional behavioral techniques of *rewards,* and *response cost.* CBT emphasizes completing *homework* as a means of changing behavior.

## SUMMARY

This manual is concerned with helping young children identify, label, and understand their feelings. The premise is that information regarding feelings can be taught. This is supported by RET and CBT . Feelings also are influenced by cognitions which can be either rational or irrational. We can teach people to identify irrational cognitions and to replace them with rational ones. The person's actions will reflect the conditions. All three—feelings, cognitions, and actions—are linked. According to Ivey (1988) "many authorities argue that our thoughts and actions are only extensions of our basic feelings and emotional experience" (p. 109). A developmental perspective would suggest that we begin by teaching feelings which will build to a greater understanding of cognitions and actions.

# Part II

# STRUCTURE

# and

# ORGANIZATION

# GROUP ESSENTIALS

**Background**

The leader needs to understand the characteristics of the age group with which they are working. A child development text or a text on childhood psychopathology can be a good refresher for many group leaders. This manual will describe briefly characteristics of children at the age levels for each designated group.

**Mechanics of Beginning**

Prior to a group beginning the leader should

1. obtain a place for the group to meet. Be certain the room is appropriate to the age, size, and number of children that are expected.

2. obtain supplies of materials to be used in group projects.

3. obtain consent from the parent (and child, dependent on age) for the child's participating in a group.

4. obtain release of information in adherence with the data privacy act.

5. be certain adequate intake has been achieved prior to a group beginning.

**Group Facilitator**

The role of the group facilitator is to serve as the organizer, planner, and leader of the group. In most classrooms the facilitator role is assumed by the teacher. At times a teaching aide or an intern may serve as a co-facilitator. The advantage of a co-facilitator is that one adult can direct the activity while the other adult monitors the emotions of the group members.

## Size

Primary aged children: 6 to 8 group members

Intermediate aged children: 6 to 10 group members

Note: As much difficulty can occur with having a group that is too small as in having a group that is too large. A small group can be difficult to obtain interaction between members.

## Session Topics

Sample lesson plans are provided for primary and intermediate age groups. Some worksheets are provided to use in the group sessions. You may add activities or modify them. As a group leader gains experience, it is likely he/she will find "favorite" activities.

Topics for discussion are provided for the group members. You will have to assess your group; however, many older children enjoy projects/activities designed for their age group as an auxiliary to discussion.

## Termination

1. Prior to the last session be sure to inform the group that next week is the last session.

2. The last session is a good time to ask the group to describe what they have learned.

3. The group should be evaluated by group members, parents, and facilitators.

4. Parent newsletters can be sent out at the end of the group. The newsletter is to inform parents of how the

group went and topics covered. If another group is to be offered, that information can be included.

# STAGES OF GROUP DEVELOPMENT

Research in group development (Corey & Corey, 1982; Schmuck & Schmuck, 1979) has indicated that groups tend to evolve through certain stages. Group leaders should be aware of these stages as they effect the nature of tasks that can be accomplished in a group setting. The groups discussed in this manual are specific and limited. In other words, the group experience has a focal goal which will be defined, examined, worked through, and resolved. *Therefore, the groups in this manual are designed to be short term interventions and/or support groups.* They are not intended to replace more intensive therapy for the individual who may need indepth examination of certain areas of his/her life. Trotzer (1989) had developed 5 stages of group process: security, acceptance, responsibility, work, and closing (termination). These stages will be discussed briefly in this section. Trotzer's (1989) work is referred to as well as the earlier work of Corey and Corey (1982) and Schmuck and Schmuck (1979).

## Security Stage

The security stage of a group has been called the initial state. It will set the atmosphere, goals, and limitations of the group. Children will need for group leaders to facilitate all members becoming acquainted. A group begins forming cohesiveness as group members find safe ways to begin to express feelings and thoughts. In many cases members will be more willing to express facts about themselves (e.g., name, age, school, pets, likes, dislikes). Leaders should structure initial exercises so that group members learn to express feelings, thoughts, and attitudes. To meet this end group leaders should model these behaviors (e.g., "I sometimes feel sad when it rains all day." This sentence is more appropriate to a feelings group than "It has sure rained a lot lately.").

A major task in the security stage is for the group to **develop trust.** Naturally group members will be cautious in self-expression when they do not know other group members. Often group members feel awkward and are unsure of whether or not becoming more involved is safe. Group members are uncertain as to whether they want to become involved. Trust is established as members get acquainted, begin to take more risks, work at establishing common ground. The group builds an atmosphere of confidentiality. Leaders can model respect, caring, acceptance, and empathy. Often trust can be established more quickly when the issue of mistrust is discussed. Trotzer (1989) believed that trust is the most dynamic experience members gain from the group. Trust is a basic human need for security. As members feel secure they can discuss positive experiences, fear, and negative feelings. Members need to learn that they can safely express feelings and leaders should encourage sharing of positive and negative feelings.

The security stage is characterized by **establishing group norms,** or **rules.** Children typically will not have participated in other structured groups. They may come to the group with preconceived, or implicit, expectations regarding the nature of the group that are based on classroom experiences. Leaders need to take responsibility for leading a discussion about the rules of the group. In general, groups function well if they have approximately five rules. Children will be aware of rules that are in effect in their classrooms and will often suggest those rules for the group. Leaders need to facilitate the discussion of the *concepts of confidentiality of group information and empathy and respect for each other.* For example, with the primary grade children rules may be stated as follows: "no put downs." "No talking about the group out of the group."

In summary, the initial stage of the group will

1. set rules and limitations,

2. teach members what to expect from group,

3. develop trust, and

4. set group goals.

## Acceptance Stage

The acceptance stage of a group is related to the human need for belonging (Trotzer, 1989). Members struggle to maintain personal safety and to accept the group as a safe environment in which they want to belong and to share. If a group continues to "play it safe," then most likely they will not engage in the growth process of the group experience. The group must become cohesive so that members desire to belong. Therefore, a leader must engage in behaviors that help to decrease anxiety and defensiveness. An initial aspect of this would be for the leader to respond to the feelings of the participants. Essentially, this requires the leader to observe the group members verbal and nonverbal actions. When a group member makes a statement regarding a feeling, an important procedure is to recognize (e.g., label) the feeling and respond to the feeling. For example, the leader could say "I hear you saying that . . . " or "Tell me more about . . . " These responses serve to **encourage the recognition of feelings** and to reinforce the concept that feelings are important to talk about. The leader helps the members recognize feelings so that members accept or own those feelings. Members who feel acceptance from the group can continue to work on accepting aspects of their own lives.

The leader's role is a blend of **encouraging and confronting** group members. In this stage the leader is active and works at shaping the behavior of participants. This requires the leader to encourage expression of feelings, confront the group when feelings are being denied, and expressing his/her own feelings. At times the leader may need to make statements about the group's attitude or progress and to ask the group to respond to that statement. This practice is similar to setting up "straw men" to see if they are knocked down. In a group of children the leader can organize activities in a way to maximize interaction of group members. One example of this is in the use of materials for projects. In the initial stage sufficient materials need to be available for each child to work on his/her project. The result of each person's work is shared with the group. The result of their work is shared with the group.

In the acceptance stage, the leader can organize a project so that the children must share materials. The interaction of the child will serve to lessen anxiety and increase cohesiveness. The leader must be prepared to deal with confrontations and disagreements regarding the sharing of materials. Results of the projects can be shared with the group. However, the process rather than the product is of primary importance at this stage. Older children can work in pairs in order to facilitate cohesiveness.

## Responsibility Stage

The responsibility (Trotzer, 1989) stage of a group is characterized by a willingness to discuss problems relevant to the focus of the group. The group then works on **finding ways to resolve problems.** Members work together and provide support to one another as each person attempts to resolve his/her problems. The group will monitor within the developmental limitations of members; thus the leader's role as standards bearer or disciplinarian will diminish during the responsibility stage. In this stage of a group the participants should be more willing to discuss their experiences and their feelings. They should bring examples of results of their practice of or thoughts about new skills that will demonstrate the group participation is developing. Members meet needs for self-esteem and acceptance by group when they take personal responsibility for working toward resolution of their individual problems. The leader must continue to reinforce the group members for trying to put into practice new skills and behaviors. The leader should model giving suggestions to members and should encourage members to give suggestions to each other.

Another important role of the leader is to keep the group on-task, or to keep focusing the discussion. As the group becomes more comfortable with each other, a tendency is to get off the topic. The leader needs to be responsible for making statements like "It seems we are moving away from our task today . . ." or (with young children) "There will be free time later, now we need to do our work . . ."

## Work Stage

In the work stage, members give and receive help in problem solving. New skills are practiced and feedback obtained from the group members. This stage truly exemplifies the "work" of group process. Leaders can facilitate this stage by using **role-plays** and **discussions.** In these activities the group resembles society but remains safe for the members. Success in problem solving and skill practice boosts members self-confidence which, in turn, gives members the courage to try new behaviors in the broader sphere of life.

## Closing Stage/Termination Stage

The last task of the group is for members to **transfer new learning to everyday situations.** Leaders encourage members to try-out new behaviors. This task began during the responsibility and work stages; in the closing stage it is the primary focus. At this stage is when new learning needs to be made explicit so that members understand the importance and the relevance of what they have learned. This manual has a focus on learning to identify and express one's emotions. Part of this learning has an implicit agenda of making a decision. In the final stage of the group, the leader should help members to express steps they take in decision making. Essentially, members have been doing this throughout the group experience. In the final closing stage importance is placed upon the cognitive work of understanding what they have been doing during the past several months. One effective tool is to simply ask members to continue to bring to the group everyday examples that utilize what they learn in the group. As the individual describes the situation, his/her feelings, and his/her response, the leader can ask the individual to explain and clarify how he/she decided upon his/her course of action. As several members describe their activities and course of action, the leader can ask the group to make generalizations about "how they decided," or their process of problem solving. For example, the leader could compliment the child on his/her choice; and perhaps point out many alternatives could have been chosen. The group could participate in a discussion about making choices when multiple alternatives are available.

In the closing stage, the leader and participants should spend some time valuating the group experiences. The leader will have notes on the content of each group which can serve as an evaluation of group content. Participants can be asked to identify what they learned in the group. Parents can be asked for their reactions to their child's experiences as a group participant. In addition, group leaders can arrange for individual meetings with parents and their child to make specific suggestions on how to apply specific skills in everyday life.

# BASIC SKILLS FOR GROUP LEADERS

Group leaders of support groups such as the "Feelings Groups" have a certain purpose of providing support and teaching the "Feelings Are Real" curriculum. They do not provide therapy or give suggestions about the client's life. Leaders use major counseling techniques such as *listening, reflecting feelings and meaning, encouraging, open-ended questions,* and *focusing the communication.* These counseling techniques are used in all stages of group development. These skills are important for group leaders but cannot guarantee a successful group. Other qualities exist that are central to group leadership but must come from within the group leader. These qualities are *genuine caring* for group members, *positive support, positive enthusiasm,* and *welcoming* extended to each group member.

## Listening

Group leaders need to listen to what is said verbally and in tone, expression, and body movement. This is achieved by attending wholly to the person speaking. The leader attends and listens to the group as well as monitors the responses of other group members.

## Reflecting

The major function of reflecting is to make each group member's feelings, emotions, and meaning explicit and clear to the member (Ivey, 1988). Reflecting helps the person to identify his/her feelings clearly. At times the person may feel two seemingly opposing feelings simultaneously. The person may recognize the ambiguity and not be able to understand it and, therefore, be unable to take action. Ivey (1988) provided some ideas for therapists learning to use reflecting. These are valuable to the group leader as well. Some examples include

1. "I hear you say you feel . . ." (p. 110),

2. "Looks like you're happy" (p. 111), and

3. "Sally, you appear both glad and sad . . ." (p. 111).

Group leaders can adapt these type of statements as they learn the skill of reflecting.

The group leader can *reflect the meaning* that underlies a statement. When members understand their meaning, they can begin to understand their values. The group leader must be careful in the use of *reflection of meaning* in the support group. It should be used sparingly. Yet, it can be valuable in helping a child understand, for example, divorce or death. In some ways reflection of meaning tries to tap into what the *CBT*'s call *self-talk,* or all those messages the person is telling to the self. Reflection clarifies the self-talk and may help the individual understand the underlying assumptions. The use of reflection often is a paraphrase of the member's words with emphasis on the main words and/or meaning. The group leader can use sentence stems (followed by the individual's words) like: "You mean . . .," "You seem to care about . . .," "You appear to value . . ." Reflection of meaning takes into consideration the uniqueness of the person and the recognition that our underlying meaning (or *CBT*'s *self-talk*) guides our behavior.

**Encouraging**

Group leaders use encouraging to assist members in continuing to talk. Encouraging can be non-verbal such as a nod or facial expressions. Leaders can be more active in using encouraging. Basic, verbal encouraging would be the use of "um-um," "uh-huh," "yes," or "I see." Leaders can use one or few words combined with a questioning tone to keep the group member talking, such as "sad?".

## Open-ended Questions

Group leaders will ask questions and they will not want to be seen as an "Inquisitor." You can easily tell if you are using "Inquisitor" questions: group members will stop talking and say only yes or no. Questions that tend to lead to yes or no or short answers are considered closed questions and should be used sparingly and to elicit specific pieces of information. The type of question that is conducive to group is the open-ended question. The open-ended question (Ivey, 1988) encourages "others to talk and provide you with maximum information. Typically, open questions begin with how, why, or could" (p. 53). For example the leader could say "Could you give me more information . . . ?" or "Tell me why you think the divorce happened."

## Focusing

A group leader uses focusing to keep the members on the topic and to direct the group to the areas of concern.

Many statements that group members make will have multiple possible interpretations. The leader could choose from skills described in this section. Leaders will need to make choices as they respond to a multi-layered statement. These choices will be made based upon both individual and group needs. For example, the leader may focus on meaning, feeling, or encouraging. Leaders may choose to ask more questions to reach greater clarity. In a group setting the leader needs to be concerned with the individual and the group and may choose to do this by asking the group "Would any one share any personal feelings (or experiences) about what Sara has just said?" The leader may wish to follow this type of interaction by referring to concepts that have been taught in the group. For example, the leader may say "Do you remember when we talked about anger? We talked about how angry includes many feelings. Let's think of the many feelings we have just described as part of Sara's angry feelings."

## Summary of Skills

Group leaders need to practice these basic skills. Skills need to be seen as interwoven. Leaders can increase their skills by co-leading with someone who is willing to be helpful and provide feedback during this learning process. Remember these skills cannot be separated from the individual personality of each group leader. Again, the purpose of a group is to support and teach the feelings curriculum—not to provide therapy.

# FORMING GROUPS

## Starting a Group

This section on forming groups is intended to provide a general outline of how you can start a group. Groups can be found in various settings such as community agencies, public health nursing, and church settings. The information presented can be considered a beginning point for the professional starting a group. Generally a helpful procedure is to start small and later expand. Those professionals involved may wish to seek further information from further reading, workshops, and in-service activities.

## Understanding Sources of Support

One can conceptualize in almost all settings a group could be formed and it would have multiple layers of support. Each layer is interwoven with the other layers. Each layer provides a different level of support for groups and the initial movement toward forming groups can come from any layer.

For a school setting, the multiple layer concept is presented in Figure 1. The push on emphasis for forming the group could begin with any one layer or combination of layers.

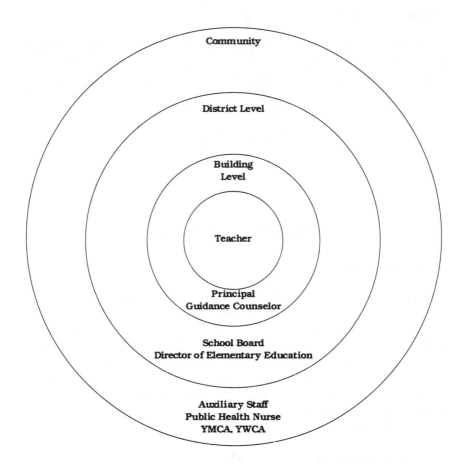

Community

District Level

Building
Level

Teacher

Principal
Guidance Counselor

School Board
Director of Elementary Education

Auxiliary Staff
Public Health Nurse
YMCA, YWCA

Starting Groups in a School:
Sources of Support

**Figure 1.** Multiple layer concept within a school.

## Guidelines for the Proposal

When you design your proposal to form "Feelings Groups" the following guidelines will be helpful:

1. describe clearly your rationale, goals, and purposes (In this manual are described curriculum and goals for primary and intermediate age children.);

2. specify the procedures to be used;

3. specify length of group;

4. specify the evaluation of the group;

5. specify how children will be selected to participate; and

6. obtain parental permission for children to participate.

## Commitment to be a Group Leader

Corey and Corey (1982) described characteristics of a group leader as being composed of personal and professional qualifications. They feel the **personal** aspects of a group leader include courage, willingness to teach by example, empathy, caring for others, encouraging people to risk and supporting them when they risk, ability to cope with the emotional attacks of group members, honesty, ability to laugh at one's self, an ability to be spontaneous, and flexible. The leader has personal qualities which assist them as a professional.

Corey and Corey felt that **professional** aspects of the group leader include many aspects. The leader needs a firm grasp of understanding of the developmental stage of the group members. The leader needs an ability to utilize good counseling skills. Leaders of a group need experience working with the age of child in the group. Leaders need to have knowledge of the research about the issues with which they deal in a group. Leaders must maintain professional ethical standards. Many professions have well-established ethical codes. Leaders need to adhere to the standards of these codes.

**Who can be a leader?** A school system has two primary sources of group leaders—teachers and auxiliary staff (school psychologists, school social workers, counselors, speech clinicians, and nurses). I know of districts where school principals have been leaders. Auxiliary staff often find that a group is an effective way of serving larger numbers of children. Teachers find that a group can be an effective activity for small groups of children. When children are selected carefully for each group, the added benefit is of increasing classroom unity. Leading a group is a way for professionals to find creative outlets and to renew their enthusiasm and caring for students. The "Feelings Are Real" curriculum is flexible and allows itself to be utilized in different settings for varying lengths of time. These qualities help the professional begin the task of leading a group.

## Classroom Groups

A group needs a set of common tasks and a shared goal. To some extent the classroom meets these characteristics. When we talk about a group that influences its members in the realm of feelings then we need to add more qualifiers for group membership. Students in a classroom are likely to have strong ties to their peer group. Leaders need to be sensitive to alliances in peer groups as they form class groups. Schmuck and Schmuck's (1979, pp. 33-50) discussion of groups applies to the peer group. These authors looked at different theories of groups and stressed that group members must

1. feel included which occurs slowly and by piece-by-piece disclosure of interests in common,

2. feel shared responsibility in developing group rules or norms (Members try to determine how much influence they can have over each other and the group. Each member needs a level of responsibility that fits their style.), and

3. feel compatible with group members, goals, and tasks.

The group leader needs to facilitate the group so that all three aspects can occur. To help a student feel included the group leader can develop introduction procedures, help students talk to each other, set-up situations so that students can learn more about each other, and demonstrate sensitivity to students' feelings by using good listening skills. Leaders can help students develop "ownership" of group rules by encouraging and assisting students as they develop rules for group and by helping students learn to monitor themselves. Finally, leaders can assure that members feel compatible with group goals and tasks by defining the group's work in a careful and systematic way.

## LEARNER OUTCOMES

The small group provides a safe place in which children can validate their thoughts and feelings. The group simulates the child's peer group by providing feedback about individual's thoughts and behaviors. The child can practice behavior in the group. Successful behaviors can be transferred to the child's larger environment. All positive experiences will provide opportunity for enhancing self-esteem. The following five points describe specific outcomes obtained by group members. The group experience is a learning experience and, therefore, this section is called "Learner Outcomes."

1. Children will learn that they can **rely on other people** to help them explore issues. They will learn that

    a. all people make choices (problem-solving skills);

    b. all groups have rules and consequences for breaking the rules;

    c. support is available from family, friends, school, community, and church; and

    d. sometimes to get what you want necessitates waiting (deferred gratification).

2. Children will learn **appropriate ways to express their feelings.** They will learn that

a.  all people experience many different feelings,

b.  the way we feel will influence the way we act,

c.  most people want to feel good and will try to behave in a variety of ways to maximize the chance of feeling good, and

d.  we all make mistakes.

3. Children will learn **decision-making skills.** They will learn that

a.  most problems have many different answers,

b.  a person must choose to behave in ways that fit with his/her values, and

c.  the good and bad of all decisions can be analyzed.

4. Children will **experience support.** They will learn that

a.  we can ask for help or for support,

b.  we have the ability to give and receive support,

c.  we all have different strengths and weaknesses,

d.  people are important, and

e.  communication is very important.

5. Children learn that they *can take risks and make changes.*

# Part III

## MANUAL

### for

## PRIMARY WORKBOOK

### Grades 2 and 3

# MANUAL FOR PRIMARY WORKBOOK

## INTRODUCTION

The developmental stage of children in the primary group is considered the latency period by Freud and the industry versus inferiority crisis by Erikson. The child is ready to work and to accomplish. The child wants to meet standards of success not just explore tasks. In Piaget's theory of cognitive development the child is making the transition from the Preoperational period (ages 2 to 5 or 7) to the Concrete Operations period (ages 7 to 11). This means that the child can use symbols in his/her play. The child is able to play with symbols. The child is watchful and imitates behaviors observed. In most cases the child is egocentric in that only one point of view can be held at one time. This will begin to change in concrete operations as the child becomes a more flexible thinker. Flexibility can be enhanced if the child is helped to learn about other people's thinking and points of view.

In the primary age group, children are becoming socialized. The child becomes increasingly influenced by peers. Rules have a great deal of authority without regard as to the source of the rule. The young child appears to feel that "a rule is a rule, is a rule . . ." As the child experiences cognitive growth, changes will occur in the perception of the rule. These changes are the result of interacting with others, imitating them, learning their rationale for their behavior. For example, children can take the role of one whose moral judgement is at a slightly higher level of development. In doing this the child learns and grows. Smart and Smart (1978) stated that children ask themselves several questions as they try to understand another point of view. These questions are

"1. Does the other see something? 2. Does the other see the same thing I see or something different? 3. What exactly is it that he sees? 4. How does it appear to him?" (p. 205). The child is addressing what the other person sees and feels. This type of experience helps the child grow in the ability to understand social roles. The ability to image another's viewpoint allows the child to develop deep friendships. Throughout the school year the child continues to develop an understanding of other's roles and increases in the ability to communicate.

Children develop their sense of self-esteem from both their own and others' evaluations of their work. When the child's achievements meet or exceed his/her belief regarding ability, then the child feels good about the self and this contributes to high self-esteem. Easily one can see how performance in school contributes to self-esteem. Another source of evaluation of the child is from important adults in the child's life. The supportive presence of adults can assist the child in coping with life changes. *Group leaders have the ability to be important adult figures.* To develop positive self-esteem the primary group leader must use positive encouragement to direct a child's efforts at a task. The group leader enhances self-esteem by focusing on positive strengths in each child.

## GROUP SESSIONS

Ten group sessions are presented for the Primary Level. (See Figure 2.). The 10-sessions can be completed

1. one session per week,

2. one session completed over several weeks, or

3. ten sessions completed during the semester with sessions and activities spaced.

The program is designed to be flexible. In order to help leaders spend time with group members the manual is organized for ease of use. First, the session will be described including purpose(s), session openings, discussion topics, session closings,

## Primary Group

| Session Number | Topic | Activities |
|---|---|---|
| 1. | Introduction | 1A. Name Tags<br>1B. My Favorite Activity<br>1C. Meet . . . Me! |
| 2. | Rules | 2A. Rules, Rules<br>2B. Catch the Closing |
| 3. | Sharing Feelings | 3A. Color Square<br>3B. Feelings Tags<br>3C. Feelings Alphabet<br>Draw a Feeling<br>3D. Sharing<br>3E. Share, Draw, and Tell |
| 4. | Happy and Sad | 4A. Draw a Face<br>4B. Discussion of Happy and Sad<br>4C. Warm Fuzzies and<br>Cold Pricklies |
| 5. | Afraid and Worried | 5A. Afraid<br>5B. Worry<br>5C. Afraid Balloons<br>5D. Grab a Feeling |
| 6. | Anger | 6A. My Mad-ometer<br>6B. Draw Anger<br>6C. Anger Away<br>6D. Anger Dragon |
| 7. | Stress | 7A. Too Much Work—<br>Too Little Time |
| 8. | Relaxation | 8A. 4-ways to Relax<br>8B. New Way to Relax |
| 9. | Friendship | 9A. Being a Friend<br>9B. 4 Square Share<br>9C. Music<br>9D. Sharing |
| 10. | Self-concept | 10A. Unique You<br>10B. Life Line<br>10C. Goodbye<br>10D. Autographs |

**Figure 2.** Topics and activities for primary school level children listed by sessions.

and session evaluation. This information is intended to be used with each activity for that session. Activities are designed to be self-contained. That is, the leader can use one or more activities for each session. The leader may choose to use all activities for a session but complete them one per week. *All activities are intended to last 20 to 25 minutes.* Leaders can vary the length of each session by varying the number of activities included.

## FEELINGS GROUP FOR PRIMARY AGE CHILDREN

**AGE LEVEL:** 2nd and 3rd grade children (may be extended downward to the last half of 1st grade)

**SIZE:** 6 to 8 children

**PURPOSES:** To identify and to express feelings. To share feelings with other participants.

**DURATION:** One hour once a week for 10 sessions or 20-minutes once a week for 10 to 25 sessions

**STRUCTURE:** Each session will include information about the purpose, session openings, exercises, discussion topics, session closings, and session evaluation. Activities are listed after each session. Leaders may select any number of activities for use in group.

✳        ✳        ✳        ✳

# SESSION 1

# INTRODUCTION

## Purposes

1. To provide a setting in which children can meet one another.

2. To help group members learn about each other.

## Session Opening

This session opens with play activities. Play allows group members to feel comfortable and safe. Play is a natural way that children make friends.

## Activity 1A: NAME TAGS

### Objective

To have children learn each others's names. The first activity will be to make name tags. The focus of the group is on feelings and the name tags can reflect that theme by having a happy and sad side of each name tag. Direct the children to tell their names one by one to other group members seated at the table.

**Materials:** *Primary Workbook*, yarn, heavy paper, crayons or markers, tape, and scissors

### Procedure

1. Have children make name tags. (Use pages 1 and 2 in *Primary Workbook*).

2. Use tape to fasten each child's name tag onto his/her clothes.

3. Have children go around the table and tell their names.

4. Play a "game" designed to increase remembering of names. For example, "my name is Jim, my eyes are blue." The next person would say "his name is Jim, his eyes are blue: my name is Sue and my eyes are brown." This process would continue all around the group.

## Discussion Ideas

After group members introduce each other the leader should discuss one of these questions.

1. "What would you do to meet other kids if you had to start attending a new school?"

2. "What can you do to help a new kid meet people in your class?"

## Evaluation

See how well the children learned each other's names by going around and having the rest of the children as a group say each successive child's name.

## Activity 1B: MY FAVORITE ACTIVITY . . .

### Objective

To complete worksheet 1B in order to have each child share his/her worksheet with another group member. Group members will introduce each other's favorite activity.

**Materials:** *Primary Workbook*, and pencil or crayon

### Procedure

1. Explain Activity 1B in the workbook (i.e., "Today we are going to identify our favorite activity and then share with others in our group").

2. Have the children do items 1 and 2.

3. Ask each child to identify his/her favorite activity.

4. Have the children draw on the back side of Activity 1B sheet a picture of their favorite activity in the past week.

5. Have the children share their work.

### Discussion Ideas

Help members share how it felt when they learned someone else had the same "Favorite things."

### Evaluation

See how well the children shared their favorite activities by asking their group members to tell what they learned about the other members.

### Activity 1C: MEET . . . ME!

#### Objective

To focus on identifying special aspects of each student in order to help the group members learn about each other.

**Materials:** Primary *Workbook* and crayon or pencil

#### Procedure

1. Explain Activity 1C in the Primary *Workbook* (i.e., "Today we are going to share some special things about ourselves such as our names, color of our hair, etc").

2. Have the children individually complete each item (1a through 1b) as the leader reads the questions.

3. Assign group members to work in pairs. Have them share information from the worksheet.

4. Call an end to the first pair and have children re-group in pairs. This allows children to get to know more members.

## Evaluation

Ask for volunteers to see how many children can name a special aspect of all the other children with whom they worked.

## Session Closings

Have children tell the group one thing they learned today.

## Session Evaluation

| | |
|---|---|
| 5 = almost always | 2 = seldom |
| 4 = sometimes | 1 = not really |
| 3 = 50/50 | 0 = not covered, not learned |

Questions to rate 0 to 5:

\_\_\_\_\_  1. Did group members learn each other's names?

\_\_\_\_\_  2. Did group members show interest in completing the activity?

\_\_\_\_\_  3. Did group members volunteer ideas?

\_\_\_\_\_  4. Did group members ask for help in an appropriate way?

**Brief Comment** _____

_____

_____

_____

✳        ✳        ✳        ✳

# SESSION 2

## RULES, RULES

### Purposes

1. To establish rules that will guide the group sessions.

2. To continue to increase the trust and sharing among group members.

### Session Opening

This session begins by reviewing names. The group leader can ask members to share something special that happened since the first meeting.

### Activity 2A: RULES, RULES

#### Objective

To help members share rules that already exist in the classroom.

**Materials:** *Primary Workbook* and pencil

#### Procedure

1. Direct children to write classroom rules.

2. Discuss these rules.

3. Work as a group to develop rules for group.

4. Suggested rules include

   a. no running,

   b. keep hands and feet to yourself,

   c. stay in the room,

d.   no shouting, and

e.   one person talks at a time.

### Discussion Ideas

1. Have members discuss why rules are important.

2. Lead a discussion about confidentiality.

   a.   Define the term.

   b.   What is said within the group, stays in the group.

3. Discuss what we will do if someone breaks the rules.

### Evaluation

See how many new rules the group can develop.


### Activity 2B:  CATCH THE CLOSING

#### Objective

To help the children review Session 1 and to learn more about each other.

**Materials:** *Primary Workbook*; soft, small ball or beanbag; and pencil.

#### Procedures:

1. Ask the children to hold hands and form a circle.

2. Have them stay in the circle and drop hands.

3. Give one of the members a soft, small ball or beanbag.

4. Ask the person with the item that is to be thrown to address questions such as

"My name is _____, I have _____ brothers"

"My eyes are what color?"

5. After raising the questions, have the person toss the ball or bag to someone else in the group who is to give the answer. The unexpected aspect of who will catch the toss helps make this a game-like atmosphere.

6. Have that person then to repeat Steps 4 and 5.

7. Have the children answer the questions in the *Primary Workbook* about the Activity.

**Session Evaluation**

| | |
|---|---|
| 5 = almost always | 2 = seldom |
| 4 = sometimes | 1 = not really |
| 3 = 50/50 | 0 = not covered, not learned |

Questions to rate 0 to 5:

_____ 1. Did group members learn each other's names?

_____ 2. Did group members show interest in completing the activity?

_____ 3. Did group members volunteer ideas?

_____ 4. Did group members ask for help in an appropriate way?

**Brief Comment:** _____

_____

_____

_____

_____

✳        ✳        ✳        ✳

# SESSION 3

## SHARING FEELINGS

### Purposes

1. To facilitate sharing among group members.

2. To learn to identify feelings.

### Session Opening

In beginning activity, review the names of the children. One activity that can be used is to have the children ask the person next to them "What is your favorite color?" (Activity 3A). Then each individual can introduce the person next to him/her along with his/her favorite color. The workbook allows the child to color a square for each neighboring child.

### Activity 3A:  COLOR SQUARE

#### Objectives

1. To help children share non-threatening information.

2. To help children learn how to request information from other people.

**Materials:**  *Primary Workbook* and crayons

#### Procedure

1. Discuss colors and how each of us generally have a favorite color.

2. Ask each child to identify his/her favorite color and write the name in the *Workbook*.

3. Direct children to color the top square their favorite color.

4. Arrange the children in a circle and teach them how to request information from the child on both sides of themselves.

5. Model making an introduction. For example, the leader can say "Hi, my name is Ms. Smith. What is your name?" Then the leader could say "Do you have a favorite color? My favorite color is purple."

6. Have the children introduce themselves to the person on their left and their right.

7. Have them write the person's name and color the person's favorite color in the square in the *Workbook*.

8. Then have them introduce the person to their right.

### Evaluation

See how well the children learned how to request information and introduce themselves.

### Activity 3B: FEELING TAGS

#### Objectives

1. To introduce happy and sad feelings.

2. To help children learn names.

3. To help children learn that sharing is valued by the group.

**Materials:** *Primary Workbook*, crayons, scissors, and tape

#### Procedure

1. Read with the children the top part of Activity 3B in the *Workbook*.

2. Have each child color the face that tells how he/she feels today.

3. Have them cut out the colored face.

4. Help them tape the colored face onto themselves.

5. Have each child say the names of the child on the left side and the one on the right side so as to review names.

6. Ask them to complete Activity 3B in the *Workbook.*

**Evaluation**

Determine how well they can identify differences between happy and sad feelings. Also try to determine the extent to which they begin to have an appreciation for sharing of feelings.

**Activity 3C: FEELINGS ALPHABET—DRAW A FEELING**

**Objectives**

1. To emphasize the number of different feelings that are available.

2. To explain that many feeling words have similar meanings (i.e., afraid, scared).

**Materials:** *Primary Workbook* and crayons

**Procedure**

1. With the children review the list of feelings with the alphabet and help them discuss the different feelings.

2. Tell children to draw a face on each of the top 3 circles. Each face should show a different feeling.

3. Have children share their drawings with the group.

4. Instruct children to listen when other group members share feeling drawings.

5. Instruct children to draw new feeling faces on the bottom 2 circles. Each child should have 5 different feeling faces after the group concludes the sharing.

**Evaluation**

See how many different feelings the children drew on their faces and determine which ones where the most popular.

**Note:** A feelings poster can be purchased from (a) How you feel today? P.O. Box 1085, Agoura, CA 91301 and (b) How are you feeling today? Creative Therapy Associates, Inc., Cincinnati, Ohio.

## Activity 3D: SHARING

**Objective**

To discuss the various ways we share activities, feelings, toys, food, work, etc.

**Materials:** *Primary Workbook* and pencil

**Procedure**

1. Read aloud the storybook entitled *What does it mean? Sharing* (Riley, 1978d) or from another book such as those listed in the reference list where the emphasis is on sharing.

2. Discuss the book *What does it mean? Sharing* or some other book, story or article on the topic of sharing.

    a.  What does it mean "to share?"

    b.  Tell one way you and your family share.

    c.  How can you share at school?

    d.  When is it okay not to share?

3. Discuss the many different feelings that people have and that sometimes to express how we feel is not easy. Emphasize that if we talk about our feelings, we are more likely to be able to label our feelings.

4. Have the children to look at the picture in the *Workbook.*

5. Have children discuss what is happening.

6. Direct student to tell how each child feels.

7. Have children tell how those in the picture share.

8. Help children write a definition of share.

9. Have the children volunteer to read their definitions to the group.

10. See how many different definitions they can make.


**Evaluation**

Based on definitions shared, determine whether or not the children are internalizing the true meaning of sharing.

## Activity 3E: SHARE, DRAW, AND TELL

### Objective

To create a picture that shows sharing and then to tell the group about the picture.

**Materials:** *Primary Workbook* and crayons

### Procedure

1. Instruct children to think of something they wish to share.

2. Have the children draw the image they wish to share.

3. Instruct the group to tell a continuous story that links each child's picture with the rest of the group.

### Evaluation

Determine how well the children understood the concept of sharing by seeing how long they can continue the story.

If additional practice relating to feelings is needed, have group members take turns (or use "Catch the Closing" procedures for Session 2) saying names and a new feeling learned today.

## Session Evaluation

| | |
|---|---|
| 5 = almost always | 2 = seldom |
| 4 = sometimes | 1 = not really |
| 3 = 50/50 | 0 = not covered, not learned |

_____ 1. Did group members learn each other's names?

_____ 2. Did group members show interest in completing the activity?

_____ 3. Did group members volunteer ideas?

_____ 4. Did group members ask for help in an appropriate way?

**Brief Comment:** _____

_____

_____

_____

_____

✳          ✳          ✳          ✳

# SESSION 4

# HAPPY AND SAD

## Purposes

1. To facilitate the labeling of and expression of feelings.

2. To enhance the interaction of the group members.

3. To affirm the use of happy and sad.

## Session Opening

Help the children to recognize that during the session they will continue with feelings as in Session 3. First, they will examine different feelings and, then, second, they will examine two specific feelings—happy and sad.

## Activity 4A: DRAW A FACE

### Objective

To provide an activity that will review the feelings learned in Activity 3C.

**Materials:** lunch bag, feelings written on strips of paper, and crayons.

### Procedure

1. Use a lunch bag that contains feelings words written on individual pieces of paper. Examples of feeling words would include

| | | |
|---|---|---|
| embarrassed, | hurt, | free, |
| proud, | confused, | tense, |
| frustrated, | accepted, | down, |
| scared, | unique, | anxious, |
| angry, | bored, | clumsy, |
| guilty, | cocky, | worthless, |
| lonely, | weak, | joyful, and |
| healthy, | strong, | inadequate. |

2. Instruct children to select a feeling by picking one paper strip from the bag.

3. Ask the children to turn to the page in their workbook labelled "Draw A Face" and have each child draw a face that depicts the feeling he or she selected from the bag.

4. Instruct the children to share the "Faces" by having other group members to guess the feeling portrayed on each drawing.

**Discussion Idea**

Discuss with the children how one can have many feelings and some of the things that cause different feelings.

**Evaluation**

Decide how well they understood feelings by

1. how many of them were able to draw pictures without having to have explanations, and

2. the number who participate in the guessing of feelings portrayed.

**Activity 4B: DISCUSSION OF HAPPY AND SAD**

**Objectives**

1. To have the children recognize two specific feelings.

2. To help the children distinguish between happy and sad.

**Materials:** none

**Procedure**

1. Have the children share whether they feel happy or sad today.

2. Ask them to identify some times when they were happy and to write those in Item 1 in the *Workbook*.

3. Ask them to express in their words how they feel when happy and to write those feelings in Item 2 in the *Workbook*.

4. Ask them to identify some times when they were sad and to write those in Item 3 in the *Workbook*.

5. Ask them to identify how they feel when they are sad and to write those in Item 4 in the *Workbook*.

**Discussion Idea**

Discuss the types of wants the children identified as being related to feeling happy and sad.

**Evaluation**

Determine the extent to which they understand the concepts by how many children

1. contributed definitions.

2. were able to give illustrations of happy and/or sad.

**Activity 4C: WARM FUZZIES AND COLD PRICKLIES**

**Objective**

To describe warm fuzzies and cold pricklies.

**Materials:** *Workbook*, crayons, purchased or leader-made warm-fuzzy or cold prickly

**NOTE:** The leader can make the atmosphere more game-like by making, or buying, a fuzzy (e.g., a pom-pom for a roller skate). A reasonable item for a cold prickly can be obtained in a pet shop. The plastic pet toy looks prickly and is an abstract porcupine.

### Preparation Before Activity

1. Use a resource such as the book *T.A for Tots* (Freed & Freed, 1977) to lead a discussion about happy and sad. A well-known method of teaching some of the dimensions of happy and sad is by using Dr. Claud Steiner's concepts of "Warm Fuzzies" and "Cold Pricklies," which was used in the *T.A. for Tots* book. In fact, Dr. Steiner has written a book called "A Warm Fuzzy Tale." These are two concepts that a child in this age group seem to like and understand. Leaders should familiarize themselves with these concepts before they choose to use Activity 4C in the group. Essentially, the concepts in Activity 4C come from transactional analysis. "Warm Fuzzies" and "Cold Pricklies" are two types of strokes. A "stroke" is a transaction, or "things that people do to us that cause us to feel" (Freed & Freed, 1977, p. 8). When we feel good, it is because we have received a warm fuzzy and when we feel bad, it is because we have received a cold prickly. They also discuss receiving "Freebies," strokes you do not have to earn, but get simply for being. In general, these strokes are from people important to us, such as our parents and family members. The Freeds discussed that at times we work to get cold pricklies. This happens when we do not think we can get warm fuzzies and "any stroke is better than no stroke." Be prepared to give examples to the children. Examples that are fairly neutral include saying hello and using someone's name, giving a compliment, and smiling, or for cold pricklies, getting yelled at for spilling your milk. The group can describe these two types of strokes.

2. Before doing the activity either make or purchase a warm fuzzy and a cold prickly.

**Procedure**

1. Tell the children about "warm fuzzies," "cold pricklies," and "freebies."

2. Instruct children to think about ways that they have tried to obtain "warm fuzzies" and "cold pricklies" and write their answer in Items 1 and 2 in their *Workbooks*.

3. Ask children to share their thoughts from Procedure 2.

4. Show the class the "warm fuzzy" that you made or purchased for uses in the activity.

5. Pass, or toss, the "warm fuzzy" around and have children take turns describing "warm fuzzies". For example, the leader could say "I think a 'warm fuzzy' is _____."

6. Ask them to write answers to Item 3 in their *Workbook*.

7. Repeat Procedure 5 using the cold prickly.

8. Ask them to write answers to Item 4 in their *Workbook*.

9. Play a game using the made or purchased "warm fuzzy" and "cold prickly." Toss the item randomly to group members. When a member receives the item, he/she answers "I can receive 'warm fuzzies' if _____," or "I can avoid 'cold pricklies' if _____."

10. Have them write answers to Item 5 in *Workbook* regarding when they received freebies.

### Discussion Idea

Lead a discussion about all the ways the group discovered to obtain "warm fuzzies" and to avoid "cold pricklies."

## Session Closing

Lead a closing time by asking the children to tell three things they learned about feeling happy or about "warm fuzzies" and three things they learned about feeling sad or "cold pricklies".

## Session Evaluation

| | |
|---|---|
| 5 = almost always | 2 = seldom |
| 4 = sometimes | 1 = not really |
| 3 = 50/50 | 0 = not covered, not learned. |

Rate these questions from 0 through 5

_____  1. Is the group functioning well together?

_____  2. Is there a level of cohesiveness?

_____  3. Are you, the leader, attending to the depth of statements that members make?

_____  4. Are group members expressing feelings, increasing ways of communicating, expressing, receiving, and giving support?

**Brief Comment:** _____

_____

_____

✳        ✳        ✳        ✳

# SESSION 5

# AFRAID AND WORRIED

## Purposes

1. To introduce and teach the concepts of afraid and of worried.

2. To facilitate the discussion of feelings.

## Session Openings

1. Two books are available that have been written on this topic.

   a.  *What does it mean? Afraid.* (Riley, 1978a)

   b.  *Sometimes I'm Afraid.* (Tester, 1979)

   Reading one or both of these books will introduce these two feelings. Alternatively, the group could define **fear, frighten, afraid,** and **scared** by using the dictionary.

2. Have children complete the sentence "I would be afraid if _____."

## Activity 5A: AFRAID

### Objective

To help children describe the way they act when they are afraid.

**Materials:** *Workbook,* pencil

### Procedure

1. Discuss with the children the feeling of being afraid.

2. Have them discuss what happens when they are really afraid.

3. Have them complete Item 1 in *Workbook*.

4. Have them discuss what constructive things they could do if they are afraid.

### Evaluation

Determine how well the children understand the concept of afraid by what they share with the group.

## Activity 5B: WORRY

### Objective

To help children describe their behavior when they worry.

**Materials:** *Workbook*, pencil

### Procedure

1. Discuss with the children the feeling of being worried.

2. Read the sentence stems in the workbook, Activity 5B, Item 1, to the children and have them discuss what they do.

3. Ask them to complete in the *Workbook* Item 1.

4. Discuss with them what things they could do that would be helpful when worried.

5. Ask them to complete Item 2 in the *Workbook*.

### Evaluation

Determine how well they understand the concept of worry by what they share with the group.

## Activity 5C: AFRAID BALLOONS

### Objective

To help the children learn a technique for releasing their afraid feelings.

## Discussion

In this activity, balloons are blown up and children draw something on the balloons that make them afraid. Then when they get ready they can pop the balloon (or ask the leader to pop the balloon with a pin) and thereby confront whatever makes them afraid, share it, and finally, send it away.

**Materials:** *Workbooks*, crayons, balloons, markers, pin

## Procedure

1. Instruct children to turn to Activity 5C in the *Workbook* and ask them to answer Items 1, 2, and 3.

2. Discuss with them how they probably were or are afraid when a balloon breaks.

3. Ask them to respond to Item 4 in the *Workbook*.

4. Provide enough balloons for each child.

5. Have the balloons blown up by the children. Some of them may need assistance.

6. Have children use a marker and draw a frightening face or object on their balloon.

7. Have children think of their fear of the noise when the balloon breaks.

8. Tell them how to pop the balloon and send their fear away.

9. Pop the balloon by use of a pin. An alternate method is to have children sit on balloons to pop them. Be certain that the marker does not get on clothing.

10. Have children talk about what it was like to get enough courage to pop the balloon.

11. Discuss things they could do the next time they are afraid that might be helpful.

12. Ask them to complete Item 5 in the *Workbook*.

13. Discuss things they could do the next time they are worried that might be helpful.

14. Ask them to complete Item 6 in the *Workbook*.

### Evaluation

Listen for the children to laugh or giggle as they "pop" the balloon. This will show a release of fear. Determine if the children understand that confronting a fear helps it go away.


## Activity 5D: GRAB A FEELING

### Objective

To create a game-like atmosphere which will enhance the discussion of feelings.

**Materials:** *Workbook*, bag with feeling-words in it.

### Procedure

1. Instruct children to draw one feeling-word from the bag.

2. Write the feeling-word and its meaning (1 and 2) in the *Workbook*.

3. Have children answer 3 and 4 in *Workbook*, these questions are:

   What do you do when you are really _____ ?

   At school, if I feel _____ I would _____ .

### Discussion Ideas

Facilitate discussion of these feelings.

### Evaluation

Determine how well they understand the concepts afraid and worried by observing how many of them contribute to the discussion.

## Session Closing

Members can complete the statement "The next time I'm afraid (or leaders may use 'worried') I will _____." Children should fill-in-the-blank by naming an activity or thought that will help them if they are afraid or worried.

## Session Evaluation

| | |
|---|---|
| 5 = almost always | 2 = seldom |
| 4 = sometimes | 1 = not really |
| 3 = 50/50 | 0 = not covered, not learned. |

____ 1. Did members give support and/or suggestions to each other?

____ 2. Is the group cohesive?

____ 3. Does the group function as a unit?

____ 4. Do members have more ways to express themselves.

**Brief Comment:** _____

_____
_____
_____
_____
_____

✳        ✳        ✳        ✳

# SESSION 6

## ANGER

### Purposes

1. To explore anger and its expression.

2. To find ways to getting rid of anger.

3. To create an increased need for interaction by decreasing the variety of activities for free play and increasing free play items that necessitate interaction.

### Session Opening

1. Begin with a review of the concepts learned in Session 4 including happy, sad, "warm fuzzy," and "cold prickly," and in Session 5 including afraid and worried.

2. Share experiences from the past week and identify the feelings that accompany the experiences.

3. Keep the group focused on the task; which includes redirecting the children when they begin to exaggerate their scores.

4. Assist the children as they label their feelings. In addition, the leader can open up discussion for the group by asking questions such as "How did you share that feeling?" or "What did you do to let someone know how you felt?"

5. Introduce the topic of anger by reading a book such as *What does it mean? Anger* (Riley, 1978b). After the book, the group can discuss when they feel angry. Children should be encouraged to give examples of situations in which they feel angry. Alternately, the leader could read definitions of angry, mad, and furious from a dictionary. The group can discuss the definition of angry and discuss situations in which they feel anger.

**Discussion Ideas**

1. Discuss ways to tell if you are angry.

   "How can you tell when you are STARTING to get angry?"

2. Discuss ways to deal with anger. (See Activity 6D).

**Activity 6A: MY MAD-OMETER**

**Objective**

To focus on anger as existing upon a continuum.

**Materials:** *Workbook*, crayons

**Procedure**

1. Direct children to examine the mad-ometer in the *Workbook*, Activity 6A. Compare this to a thermometer.

2. Point out that anger can begin at frustration, move toward mad, then to furious, and finally, toward an individual boiling point (Item 1 in *Workbook*).

3. Have children color their Mad-ometer (one of the four) to the point that tells about how they feel today (Item 2 in *Workbook*).

4. Ask them to write in Item 4 in *Workbook* those things that make them mad.

**Discussion Idea**

Have the children share the types of things that make them mad.

**Evaluation**

Observe the children's responses in Procedures 3 and 4 and in the discussion. Assess the children's understanding of the degrees of anger by whether or not they used all levels of the thermometer.

## Activity 6B: DRAW ANGER

**Objective**

To depict anger by drawing a picture of an angry face to explain the idea of masking our feelings.

**Materials:** *Workbook*, crayons, scissors

**Procedure**

1. Have the children get into groups of two so they can work in pairs.

2. Have children practice making an angry face while looking at each other.

3. Ask them to draw an angry face in the *Workbook*, Item 1.

4. Share drawings and discuss how sometimes people cover-up anger by wearing a "mask."

5. Ask the children to draw a second face in the *Workbook*, Item 2, that shows another feeling besides anger.

6. Cut out the second face. Place it over the first face.

**Discussion Ideas**

First explain how the person is still angry but the "mask" tries to hide the anger. Talk about feelings that the student tries to mask.

**Evaluation**

Determine how well they understanding "masking" feelings by observing whether the "masks" show different feelings than their face.

## Activity 6C: ANGER AWAY

### Objective

To provide an activity that will help children learn to get rid of their anger.

**Materials:** *Workbook*, crayons

### Procedure

1. Have the children talk about what they do when they get angry.

2. Ask children to turn to the *Workbook*, Activity 6C, and have each child write one way to get rid of anger (Item 1).

3. Have the children draw a picture of the activity they do to get rid of anger (Item 2).

4. Have the children write one way you get rid of anger. Space is provided in the workbook.

### Discussion Idea

Talk about the calming effects of music/drawing.

### Evaluation

See how well they understand by having them share their ideas and activities.

## Activity 6D: ANGER DRAGON

### Objective

To help children find ways to make angry feelings leave.

## Discussion

The leader should facilitate and direct the session carefully. A focus should be on appropriate expression of anger, action to decrease frustration, and redirection of attention. The leader needs to discourage aggressive responses and responses which "stuff" the anger (i.e., a lack of expression).

**Materials:** *Workbook*, crayons, pencil

## Procedure

1. Explain that anger can be like a dragon if we do not deal with it.

2. Tell them to look at how the dragon's "fire" spreads. Anger can spread as well.

3. Have the children color the dragon in *Workbook*, Activity 6D.

## Discussion Ideas

1. Lead a discussion about how to get rid of anger. A first example is listed in the *Workbook*, Activity 6D "Tell someone about it." Spaces are provided for 8 more ideas.

2. Have the children find other ways to get rid of anger. For example, they can (a) ride a bike, (b) listen to music, and/or (c) play.

3. Have the children fill-in their *Workbook*s.

## Evaluation

Determine how well they understand the concept of anger by (1) how many contribute to the discussion, and (2) how many different ways they get rid of anger.

## Session Closings

Try to use the Grab A Feeling (Activity 5D). This time after the grab, ask the group one of these questions

I get angry when  _____

I can have fun and deal with my anger by  _____

## Session Evaluation

5 = almost always          2 = seldom

4 = sometimes              1 = not really

3 = 50/50                  0 = not covered, not learned.

____  1.  Did the group understand that anger exists upon a continuum?

____  2.  Could group members give examples of angry feelings?

____  3.  Do children understand the concept of "mask?" (If not, reinforce by using more examples).

____  4.  Do children understand that anger can "spread like fire" if we do not deal with it?

____  5.  Did the group discover positive ways to cope with anger?

**Brief Comment:**  _____

_____

_____

_____

_____

✳          ✳          ✳          ✳

# SESSION 7

## STRESS

### Purposes

1. To explore the concept of stress (or tension or hurrying).

2. To provide a simulated experience of stress.

### Session Openings

1. To begin with a sharing of feelings from Activities 4, 5, and 6. The leader needs to be certain that all the feelings from previous sessions are reviewed in this sharing time. At this point, the children will (probably!) remember each others names. However, the leader can reinforce the name of group members. As in the past, children can introduce the person seated to his/her side.

2. To focus on the idea of tension or stress.

3. To identify the pressures or situations that cause us to feel stress. This is basically a defining phase of the session. Children can list times in which they felt stress.

### Activity 7A: TOO MUCH WORK—TOO LITTLE TIME

#### Objective

To create a stress situation which will enable children to discuss stress and means to release stress.

#### Background Information

This simulation is intended to be a condensed version of the classroom experience. The *Workbook* provides worksheets that are grade appropriate. Through use of the worksheets, the children are to be given more "work" than they can complete in the allotted time.

The simulation is like a series of timed tests; however, the purpose is to have too brief of time intervals so that a sense of tension or frustration develops. (Caution: The leader must remain very aware of the children's level of tension. The task should produce tension, not anger.)

**Materials:** *Workbook*, pencil, timer or watch for leader.

## Procedure

1. Ask children to turn to Activity 7A in their *Workbooks*.

2. Assign the separate workbook sections one at a time.

3. Give a specific "start" and "stop" command for Item 1.

4. Continue Steps 2 and 3 until all three sections are completed.

## Discussion Ideas

1. Immediately lead a discussion about how it felt to run out of time and not be able to finish your work. The central theme should be that of tension, or stress and how we feel when we are stressed.

2. Confirm that children understand "stress" by asking them to tell you what you have said! This often is an interesting aspect of the Activity to see how children interpret the concept of stress.

3. Have them discuss possible ways to reduce stress.

## Evaluation

Determine the extent to which they understand the concept by the number who contribute to the discussion and the number of ways they devise to reduce stress.

## Session Closing

1. Group members can share that they felt stress in the classroom. Ask for specific examples.

2. Ask children to answer the question "What can you do after school if you have had "too much work— too little time" at school?"

## Session Evaluation

| | |
|---|---|
| 5 = almost always | 2 = seldom |
| 4 = sometimes | 1 = not really |
| 3 = 50/50 | 0 = not covered, not learned. |

_____ 1. Do children understand the idea of stress?

_____ 2. Were you able to produce stress—not anger— with the simulation?

**Brief Comment:** _____

_____

_____

_____

_____

✳      ✳      ✳      ✳

# SESSION 8

# RELAXATION

## Purposes

1. To introduce the concept of relaxation.

2. To illustrate the difference between stress and relaxation.

## Session Openings

1. To discuss how the temperature of our hands tells us about how we feel. That is, when our hands are cold it is likely that we are feeling stress, and when our hands are warm it is likely we are feeling relaxed. (Of course, it is important to differentiate the feeling of cold hands due to winter or cold weather). A handout can be prepared of a thermometer with the cold temperature depicting stress and the warm temperature depicting relaxation.

2. Have children volunteer examples of specific situations that make them feel stress, or "cold." It is important to emphasize that we all become tense over different things and that we all react in different ways to stress. Also emphasize that everyone feels stress and that stress if normal.

## Discussion Ideas

1. Share feelings that contrast tension with relaxation.

2. Discuss ways to reduce stress in the situations children described in Session Opening No. 2.

3. Encourage children to practice relaxation.

## Activity 8A: 4-WAYS TO RELAX

### Objective

To help children learn that a solution for stress is to learn to relax. This exercise describes 4-ways to relax.

**Material:** *Workbook*

### Procedure

1. Have the children to be seated in positions where they can practice the 4-ways to relax.

2. Have them practice for a while pretending they are a ragdoll.

3. Have them practice for a while pretending to put a ball in each hand, squeeze it, and then slowly let it roll out.

4. Have them sit cross-legged on the floor, close their eyes, take slow deep breaths, and on each exhale say "one."

5. Have them to imagine for a while that they are on the beach.

6. Have them to do Item 2 in the *Workbook*.

7. Have them discuss with each other the 4-ways to relax.

### Discussion Ideas

1. Compare each way of relaxing.

2. Emphasize that each person will find one best way to relax and that each person may be different.

### Evaluation

Did the children understand relaxation?

## Activity 8B: NEW WAY TO RELAX

### Objectives

1. To contrast tension and relaxation.

2. To teach a new way to relax.

**Materials:** *Workbook* (OPTIONAL: tape, tape recorder.)

### Procedure

1. Plan about 20 minutes to complete.

2. Instruct the children to find a place to get comfortable, such as the floor, the couch, or an easy chair. Instruct them to close their eyes and remain quiet during the reading or the tape, to listen, and to feel the relaxation. A helpful procedure is to dim the lights prior to starting the tape or reading.

3. Allow time for them to move into a comfortable position.

4. Prepare a tape ahead of time or be prepared to read to the children to help them experience relaxation. Use a soft voice and speak slowly. When you see ". . ." you should pause. "Think about your feet . . . Now point your toes . . . hold it . . . and relax your feet. Notice how your legs feel when you point your toes. Your legs feel tense. Point your toes . . . Notice the tension in your legs . . . Now relax your feet . . . See how good it feels when you relax. (Repeat pointing toes and relaxing 3 times.)

   Now, think about your arms. . . Make a fist with each hand . . . Squeeze your fists hard . . . Hold the squeeze and notice the tension in your arms . . . Relax your hands and notice how good it feels to be relaxed. (Repeat making a fist and relaxing 3 times.)

Now, point your toes . . . make fists . . . hold it . . . hold it . . . Notice the tension . . . Now relax. See how good it feels to relax.

Now, think about your head . . . Shut your eyes . . . Squeeze them shut . . . Notice how your nose feels . . . and your forehead . . . Both your nose and your forehead feel tense . . . Hold it . . . Now open your eyes and relax. Your nose and forehead feel better when you relax. (Repeat squeezing your eyes and noticing your nose and forehead 3 times.)

Now, point your toes, make fists, and squeeze your eyes . . . Hold it . . . Notice the tension Hold it Now relax. It feels so good to relax . . .

Now, think about your shoulders . . . Pull your shoulders up toward your ears . . . tighter . . . tighter. Notice the tension in your neck . . . your shoulders . . . Now relax. (Repeat 3 times.)

Now, think about your body and relax your legs . . . your arms . . . your head and face . . . your shoulders . . . Think of your whole body as relaxed . . . like a rag doll . . . very, very relaxed . . . (Allow children to stay relaxed for 2 to 3 minutes, then say . . .) I feel so-o relaxed . . . (pause 1-minute). Tell them they can slowly start to sit-up and join as a group.

5. Have them write their response to Item 4 in the *Workbook*.

6. Have them write their response to Item 5 in the *Workbook*.

7. Have them write their response to Item 6 in the *Workbook*.

8. Have them discuss the different feelings and responses to Item 4, 5, and 6.

### Evaluation

Notice the enjoyment they express when they share in Procedure Step 8.

## Session Closings

1. Discuss the contrast between tension and relaxation.

2. Discuss ways to reduce stress in several of the situations the children had described earlier in this session.

## Session Evaluation

| | |
|---|---|
| 5 = almost always | 2 = seldom |
| 4 = sometimes | 1 = not really |
| 3 = 50/50 | 0 = not covered, not learned. |

_____ 1. Were the children able to share?

_____ 2. Is the group a cohesive unit?

_____ 3. Are children participating?

_____ 4. Were children capable of understanding relaxation?

**Brief Comment:** _____

_____

_____

✳     ✳     ✳     ✳

# SESSION 9

## FRIENDSHIP

### Purposes

1. To explore the concepts of friendship.

2. To examine the requirements we have for our friends.

3. To learn ways to be a good friend.

### Session Openings

1. Describe the importance of friends by utilizing the following information.

The need to belong is considered important to all people and is included in Maslow's need hierarchy. Friendship patterns influence a child's self-esteem and ability to learn (Schmuck & Schmuck, 1979). Davis (1985) contended that friendship is a relationship between people of equal status. He has defined a cluster of characteristics of friendship including enjoyment, acceptance, trust, respect, mutual assistance, confiding, understanding, and spontaneity. The child's formation of friendships uses these characteristics at a developmentally appropriate level. Past researchers (Berscheid & Walster, 1969; Glidewell, Kanter, Smith, & Stringer, 1966; Rubin, 1973) suggested that students who are liked will be physically attractive, well-coordinated, outgoing, socially adept, academically able, and mentally healthy. Socioeconomic status may possibly influence whether a child is liked in the elementary grades. Pepitone (1964) hypothesized that interpersonal attraction depends upon other individuals assigning to the person a high status and helping them feel secure. Persons tend to validate their view of the world by checking their attitudes against the attitudes of those around them. Balance theory (Zajonc, 1960) argues that persons tend to like people who agree with their views. The development of close friendships tends to occur if people continue to find ways in which they are similar. In order for a friendship to develop generally the two children must be in proximity. Otherwise, it becomes increasingly more difficult for children to find ways to develop friendships.

2. Go directly to Activity 9A in the *Workbook.*

## Activity 9A: BEING A FRIEND

### Objectives

1. To help define the qualities of friendship.

2. To learn what we expect from our friends.

**Materials:** *Workbook,* pencil.

### Procedure

1. Have children discuss friendship and then develop a definition.

2. Have each child complete the sentence "A friend is _____" in *Workbook* Activity 9A, Item 1. The leader should encourage the children to find as many ways to fill-in-the-blanks as possible.

3. Have group members discuss ways of showing friendship.

4. Have each child complete Item 2 in *Workbook.*

5. Have group members share ways their best friends show them friendship.

6. Have each child complete Item 3 in *Workbook.*

7. Have children complete Item 4 in *Workbook.*

### Discussion Idea

Have those children who are willing to share their work talk about "best" friends.

### Evaluation

Determine if the children understand the "give and take" process of friendship.

## Activity 9B: 4 SQUARE SHARE

### Objective

To facilitate sharing, which is one quality of friendship.

### Background Information

Leaders may use the five square share puzzle concept. This task has been designed by Schmuck, Runkel, Arends, and Arends (1977) and is designed to create increased attraction and helpfulness. For example, if a group had five members, each group would be given exactly enough pieces to complete five squares. However, no individual group member is given enough pieces to complete a five square. Thus, if anyone is to complete a square, then the group must begin to cooperate. Our activity adapts this task and uses four squares.

**Materials:** *Workbook*, bag, assorted crayons

### Procedure

1. Place assorted crayons in a bag.

2. Each child will draw 1 crayon from the bag and color 1 square with that color.

3. Instruct the children to trade, or share crayons, so that every square is a different color.

4. Time the group.

5. Instruct children to answer Items 1 and 2 in the *Workbook*.

**Discussion Ideas**

1. Discuss the ideas of cooperation and sharing as qualities of friendship.

2. Discuss that it was more fun to share in order to complete this task.

**Evaluation**

If the children completed the squares, they understood sharing.

**Activity 9C: MUSIC**

**Objective**

To listen to music about friendship.

**Background Information**

One suggestion is the Marlo Thomas album called "Free to be . . . you and me."

**Materials:** album, record player, or tape and recorder, *Workbook.*

**Procedure**

1. Select song (s) to be played.

2. Have children listen to songs and complete Items 1 and 2 in *Workbook.*

3. Share the meaning of the song.

**Discussion Idea**

Talk about favorite parts of the songs.

**Evaluation**

Determine by the children's responses whether they understood the concept of sharing as portrayed in the record album.

## Activity 9D: SHARING

### Objective

To facilitate a discussion about sharing.

**Materials:** *Workbook*, crayons

### Procedure

1. Have children talk about all the t-shirts that people wear that share things.

2. Help children begin by discussing types of things we like to share, for example, favorite activities, pets, awards, hobbies, and interests.

3. Have group members describe t-shirts that they have seen that express a sharing about self, place, and others. Have each child draw in the *Workbook* a t-shirt which he/she might wear to show how he/she would share.

4. Have children show and discuss their drawings.

### Evaluation

Determine how well they understand the concept of sharing by

1. number of definitions they make, and

2. number of things they like to share.

### Discussion Ideas

1. Discuss the following topics:

   a. What would it be like to be the "new student" in school?

   b. How can we help new students make friends?

**Session Closing**

Have group discuss "I am showing friendship when _____."

**Session Evaluation**

| | |
|---|---|
| 5 = almost always | 2 = seldom |
| 4 = sometimes | 1 = not really |
| 3 = 50/50 | 0 = not covered, not learned. |

____ 1. Did the group find ways to define a friend?

____ 2. Do children understand the relationship of sharing and friendship?

**Brief Comment:** _____

_____

_____

_____

_____

✳        ✳        ✳        ✳

# SESSION 10

## SELF-CONCEPT

### Purposes

1. To build or enhance self-esteem or self-concept.

2. To terminate group.

### Session Openings

1. Discuss the meaning of self-concept. An excellent book on this subject is *100 Ways to Enhance Self-Concept in the Classroom: A Handbook for Teachers and Parents* by Jack Canfield and Harold C. Wells (1976). This book is appropriate for group leaders working with children.

   Maslow, for example, considered self-concept or self-esteem as an important need of all people. In fact, the humanist movement in psychology (for example Carl Rogers) has focused on self-concept as a critical part of the individual. To the extent that the person liked him or herself and realistically understood his or herself is the extent to which the individual was mentally healthy. A group leader could possibly conduct several group sessions which focus on self-concept.

2. Have each member share a feeling that he or she experienced during the past week.

### Activity 10A: UNIQUE YOU

#### Objective

To use a standard picture and create unique pictures.

#### Background Information

The project helps children recognize unique or special aspects of the self.

**Materials:** *Workbook,* crayons.

**Procedure**

1. Describe the worksheet as a uni-sex picture.

2. Discuss qualities that contribute to uniqueness about a person such as color of hair, length of hair, ears, nose, freckles, and number of teeth missing.

3. Instruct children to draw qualities on the outline drawing in *Workbook*, Activity 10A, which make them special or unique.

4. Complete UNIQUE YOU pictures with the group.

**Discussion Idea**

Have each child indicate one quality he or she likes about the picture. For example, the leader could model this by starting the exercise, showing his or her picture, and saying "This is I, and I like my freckles."

**Evaluation**

Observe whether each child was able to choose an aspect about his or herself that he or she liked and could share.

**Activity 10B: LIFE LINE**

**Objective**

To look at similarities and differences among group members by having each member complete a Life Line.

**Materials:** *Workbook*, pencil.

**Procedure**

1. Discuss what a Life-Line is and some meanings for making one.

2. Have students complete Life-Line worksheet in *Workbook*, Activity 10B.

3. Help students identify events and remembered dates to fill in their Life Lines by using questions such as the following:

   a. Do you remember when you got your 1st permanent tooth?

   b. When did you have measles, mumps, chicken pox?

   c. Have you ever been in the hospital?

   d. Have you moved?

   e. Do you remember a younger brother/sister being born?

   f. When did you learn to read? walk? talk? ride a bike?

   g. Do you have a favorite vacation?

   h. Have you received any awards, been in a recital, made a project for Scouts or 4-H?

   i. Others _____

4. Have students draw a star on their favorite times on their life-line.

**Discussion Idea**

Help them share ways that children are special and ways in which they are similar to others in the group.

**Evaluation**

Determine if children realize their similarities and differences.

**Activity 10C: GOODBYE**

**Objective**

To close or terminate group.

**Materials:** *Workbook*, pencil

**Procedure**

1. Ask group members to individually complete Item 1 in the *Workbook*.

2. After each has completed Item 1, have them to share.

3. Ask them to individually complete Item 2.

4. After each has completed Item 2, have them to share.

5. Ask them to individually complete Item 3.

6. After each has completed Item 3, have them to share.

7. Ask them to individually complete Item 4.

8. After each has completed Item 4, have them to share.

9. Have the children assemble into two groups and list as many feelings as they can.

10. Share feelings from the two groups.

**Evaluation**

Determine whether the children are more capable of listing feelings now as compared to the beginning of the group.

**Activity 10D: AUTOGRAPHS**

### Objective

To add a party atmosphere to the last session of group.

**Materials:** *Workbook*, pencil

### Procedure

1. Use Activity 10D as a termination of the group. If possible, have treats and a festive atmosphere.

2. Instruct children to obtain in their *Workbook*, Activity 10D, autographs from members of the group.

3. Play music in background to add to party-atmosphere.

### Discussion Idea

Ask children what they have learned about feelings.

### Evaluation

Observe whether or not the children have fun as they interact with one another.

### Session Closing

Use Exercise 10D—Autographs—as a termination of the group. It is nice to have treats and a festive atmosphere.

### Session Evaluation

| | |
|---|---|
| 5 = almost always | 2 = seldom |
| 4 = sometimes | 1 = not really |
| 3 = 50/50 | 0 = not covered, not learned. |

\_\_\_\_\_ 1. Is the sharing level of the group greater than in Session 1?

_____ 2. Did children develop ways of sharing feelings?

_____ 3. Did children find ways to give help to other group members?

**Brief Comment:** _____

_____

_____

❋          ❋          ❋          ❋

# Part IV

# MANUAL

## for

# INTERMEDIATE

# WORKBOOK

## Grades 4, 5, and 6

# MANUAL FOR INTERMEDIATE WORKBOOK

## INTRODUCTION

The developmental stage of the children in this group has been called the latency period by Freud and has been called the concrete operational period by Piaget. The children in the intermediate group are in a transitional phase of their lives. Developmentally, they are experiencing cognitive and physical changes. In addition, the style of their social relationships is changing. Physically the child becomes prepubescent during this time period and as such will experience bodily and hormonal changes. Children will vary with speed as they progress through this stage.

Cognitively, the child is in the concrete operational stage of development. Piaget referred to this stage of development as one in which the child is able to think logically and use some reasoning ability, however, to test hypotheses and understand relationships, the child needs the actual objects in front of him/her. Children's thinking styles are often reflective in that they can think about their response to an answer prior to saying it. The child understands rules and facts and at this stage the child is very concerned with obeying the rules. Kohlberg referred to this as the "good boy, good girl" level of morality. Essentially, this means that the child will display an increased sensitivity to others and will conform to the rules in order to avoid disapproval of their peers. Morality then is the process in this stage of development in which the child learns to consciously adopt standards of right and wrong.

Socially, the child is experiencing a greater need for peer relationships. The child is becoming increasingly active in interacting with other children his/her age. Essentially, the child is forming stronger friendships with same sex peers and exhibiting an increased awareness, yet not an attraction to opposite sex children. The child may worry during this developmental stage about being rejected. The child has a desire to be popular with his/her peers. At times, this can put the child at odds with his/her parents in that the child's desire to be accepted by peers may compel him/her to break parental rules if by so doing there is an increase in the likelihood that he/she would be accepted. The child becomes increasingly identified with a group of friends at this stage of development. The increasing sense of independence and ability to accomplish things on their own brings a great deal of satisfaction to the child in this intermediate age level. A current book that group leaders are recommended to read would be David Elkind's *The Hurried Child* (1981). This book describes children as they interact with the norms and expectations of society.

## GROUP SESSIONS

Ten group sessions are presented for the Intermediate Level. (See Figure 3.) The 10-sessions can be completed

1. one session per week,

2. one session completed over several weeks, or

3. ten sessions completed during the semester with sessions and activities spaced.

The program is designed to be flexible. In order to help leaders spend time with group members the manual is organized for ease of use. First, the session will be described including purpose(s), session openings, discussion topics, session closings, and session evaluation. This information is intended to be used with each activity for that session. Activities are designed to be self-contained. That is, the leader can use one or more activities for each session. The leader may choose to use all activities for a session but complete them one per week. *All activities are intended to last 20 to 25 minutes.* Leaders can vary the length of each session by varying the number of activities included.

## Intermediate Group

| Session Number | Topic | Activities |
|---|---|---|
| 1. | Getting to Know You | 1A. Name Tag Faces<br>1B. Silhouettes |
| 2. | Sharing | 2A. Autobiography<br>2B. T-Shirt Design |
| 3. | Feelings | 3A. Brainstorm<br>3B. Feelings Alphabet<br>3C. Feeling Toss |
| 4. | Assertive Behavior | 4A. Assertive Checklist<br>4B. Defining Assertion |
| 5. | Aggressive and Nonassertive Behavior | 5A. Identify Aggressive Behavior<br>5B. Identify Nonassertive Behavior<br>5C. Research Notes |
| 6. | Anger | 6A. Angry Worksheet<br>6B. Masks<br>6C. Feeling Wheel |
| 7. | My Strengths | 7A. Star<br>7B. Proud |
| 8. | Decision Making | 8A. Role-Play<br>8B. Contracts |
| 9. | Relationships—Family | 9A. Find-a-Family<br>9B. Family Description<br>9C. Family Favorites |
| 10. | Friendship | 10A. Friendship<br>10B. Special People<br>10C. Autographs |

**Figure 3.** Topics and activities for intermediate school level children listed by session.

# FEELINGS GROUP FOR
# INTERMEDIATE AGE CHILDREN

**AGE LEVEL:** 4th, 5th, and 6th grade children

**SIZE:** 6 to 10 members with a facilitator

**PURPOSES:**

1. To identify and express feelings.

2. To learn to share feelings with peers.

**DURATION:** 10 sessions for 20 to 45 minutes per session dependent upon the number of activities used.

**STRUCTURE:** In the *Leader Manual* are described the purpose(s) of each session followed by activities from which leaders can select. Leaders can use the same format for each session.

A. OPEN: Describe the goals of the group as found in the "purpose(s)" section of each session.

1. SHARE: Have the children share events and feelings from the past week.

B. MAIN ACTIVITY: Leader will select one (or more) activity from the workbook. Leader will facilitate the activity using the "procedure" section provided for that activity.

C. DISCUSS: Leader will facilitate sharing after the activity of each session.

D. CLOSING: Children will make entries in the *Workbook* during and at the end of each session. Leaders collect *Workbook*s and make brief comments prior to the next session.

✳        ✳        ✳        ✳

# SESSION 1

## GETTING TO KNOW YOU

In the intermediate group the children are given more thorough directions in the workbook. The reason for this is the increased reading level of the children. The "procedure" portion of the activity in the *Leader Manual* may refer the leader to the *Workbook*. In this case, the leader will know the *Workbook* is self-explanatory. The leader's main role is to facilitate the group and keep the group on-task.

### Purposes of Session 1

1. To provide a setting in which children learn to know each other.

2. To develop friendships within the group.

3. To have an opportunity to share unique aspects of self with the leader and/or other group members.

Remember, children in this age group will be very concerned about what other children think of them. The leader should focus on activities that help to build group cohesiveness. In addition, children need to take a great deal of pride in being creative and productive, therefore, the *leader should assure a plan so that children can remain active and productive during each group session.*

### Activity 1A: NAME TAG FACES

#### Objectives

1. To introduce happy and sad.

2. To facilitate learning names of group members.

**Materials:** *Workbook*, pencil, scissors, glue

**Procedure**

1. Described in *Workbook*

2. Leader should facilitate group process by keeping group on-task.

**Evaluation**

Determine if the children can name those persons sitting next to them.

### Activity 1B: SILHOUETTES

**Objectives**

1. To have the children work in pairs in order to get to know each other.

2. To create silhouettes of each other.

**Materials:** The group leader would need to bring a light, paper for the child's silhouette to be traced upon, scissors, magazines and/or catalog, and craft materials.

**Procedure**

1. Have the children to work together to create silhouettes of each other.

2. Have each child, by looking through magazines and catalogs, to find different pictures and words that the person feels describe him/her.

3. In addition, have the children to draw pictures and write sayings on their respective silhouettes.

4. Ask the children to work toward each having a silhouette covered with a collage of pictures and words when they are finished.

5. When finished ask the children to talk about the meaning of the collage as it relates to him/herself as a person.

   **NOTE:** Dependent on group size, this activity may take one to two sessions.

## Evaluation

1. Can each child name the other person in the group?

2. Can each child remember something specific about each group member?

**Session Evaluation:** (H = High, Λ = Average, L = Low)

(Circle one)

H  A  L     1. The children can share feelings.

H  A  L     2. The children are making positive contributions in group.

H  A  L     3. I have encouraged the children in this session.

H  A  L     4. Each child is able to write his/her feelings.

**Brief Comment:** _____

_____

_____

_____

_____

✳          ✳          ✳          ✳

# SESSION 2

## SHARING

### Purposes of Session 2

1. To increase group cohesiveness by the use of self-disclosure.

2. To give positive support and encouragement.

3. To find ways to help the group share.

### Activity 2A: AUTOBIOGRAPHY

The autobiography would be a group activity that is ultimately designed to increase self disclosure and increase risk taking for the children.

#### Objectives

1. To increase self-disclosure of important life events.

2. To encourage learning that our experiences are like the experiences of others.

**Materials:** *Workbook*, a leader prepared list of questions.

#### Procedure

1. Explain a time-line and its importance.

2. Have the children answer the leader's prepared questions about themselves by adding the information onto a time-line in the *Workbook* and, thereby create an autobiography.

3. Direct the children to share, with other group members, their autobiography summarized in time-line form.

4. Have them answer Items 4 and 5 in the *Workbook*.

**Evaluation**

1. Determine if the children understand the concept of the time-line and its importance.

2. Note how willing they are to share information with one another.

**Activity 2B: T-SHIRT DESIGN**

The goal of this activity is to share one aspect of the self with other group members. The children would share things they want, like, or hate. Essentially, the design they create should be representative of something that has meaning to them.

**Objectives**

1. To encourage sharing.

2. To help the children to identify one or more aspects of self that they are willing to share with others.

**Materials:** *Workbook*, crayons or markers

**Procedure**

1. Have the children draw on the T-shirt in Activity 2B of the *Workbook*.

2. Have them create a design for the T-shirt that will share an aspect of themselves that they would like others to know.

3. Have them share their T-shirt drawings with one another.

**Evaluation**

1. Observe whether or not the T-shirt have designs that share an aspect of each child.

2. Note how willing they are to be open, to share.

3. Have them write their answers to Items 4 and 5.

4. Collect the *Workbook*, read their comments on Activities 2A and 2B, and write "feedback" to give them at the next session.

# SESSION 3

## FEELINGS

### Purposes of Session 3

1. To help children to identify feelings.

2. To learn to label feelings.

3. To learn to find alternatives and appropriate actions that express feelings.

### Activity 3A: BRAINSTORM

#### Objectives

To brainstorm, or think of, as many feelings as they possibly can.

**Materials:** *Workbook* and pencil, or blackboard and chalk, timer

#### Procedure

1. Depending on the size of the group, if possible, divide the children into two smaller sections.

2. Set a time limit and have the two groups compete to see which group can list the most feelings.

3. Have the children write feeling words in the *Workbook*.

#### Discussion

1. After the generation of a list of feelings, have the group members to discuss the different types of feelings they identified.

2. Emphasize that all feelings are okay and that an important part of maintaining good health

is to learn constructive ways to express these feelings.

3. Find feeling words that have the same meaning.

   **Note:** A feelings poster can be purchased from (a) How you feel today? P.O. Box 1085, Agoura, CA 91301 and (b) How are you feeling today? Creative Therapy Associates, Inc., Cincinnati, Ohio.

## Evaluation

Determine how well the children understand by how many feelings they think of.

## Activity 3B: FEELINGS ALPHABET

### Objective

To think of a feeling word for each letter of the alphabet.

**Materials:** *Workbook*, pencil

### Procedure

1. Divide the group into teams.

2. Instruct each team to find a feeling-word for each letter of the alphabet.

3. Time the activity for 8 to 10 minutes.

4. Lead a sharing session for the Activity.

### Evaluation

Determine if children can find feelings for all the letters of the alphabet. If not, help the teams fill-in the alphabet by having them share among teams.

**Activity 3C: FEELING TOSS**

**Objectives**

1. To use a game to help children express how they feel.

2. To help children identify what the behaviors are that they have with specific feelings.

**Materials:** *Workbook*, scissors, pen, tape, or leader may bring two dice for each group.

**Procedure**

1. Have the children follow directions 1 through 5 in the *Workbook*.

2. Lead a discussion to help the children generate questions associated with feelings. Use their ideas as much as possible. The following are examples:

   a.  What do you do when you feel  _____

   b.  What may cause you to have the feeling of being  _____

   c.  How long does the feeling of being  _____ generally last?

   d.  What can generally change the feeling of being into a different feeling?

3. Have them make the dice (Item 10 in the *Workbook*) if they do not have dice.

4. Have them proceed with Items 7 through 9.

5. Facilitate by monitoring the group(s) as the children take turns playing the game.

6. Instruct children to write (in the *Workbook* in Item 11): "Why feelings are important."

7. Collect *Workbook*s and respond to each child in the space for Leader's Comments.

## Evaluation

1. Observe if the children cooperate with each other.

2. Evaluate the children's understanding from the writing.

# SESSION 4

## ASSERTIVE BEHAVIOR

**Purpose of Session 4**

To focus on assertive responses.

**Background Information**

Assertive behavior has been discussed by Freeman and Mesenberg (1983) in their book *Developing Group Skills.* Assertive behavior is a set of behaviors that allow an individual to express their needs and wants directly. It enables us to communicate openly and directly with others with whom we have interpersonal relationships. During this phase of the group, leaders should be especially aware of using assertive behavior in expressing their feelings, wants, and needs. By providing appropriate methods of expressing feelings and by modeling assertive behavior the leader should be able to establish a good role model for the students to follow. In addition, the leader can role play by taking the role of someone who is not using assertive behavior and see if the students can correct that behavior. Essentially, this activity involves learning the difference between assertive, non-assertive and aggressive behavior. ***Assertive behavior*** is a direct, open, and honest communication. ***Nonassertive behavior*** can be manipulative, shy, timid, and/or whining. ***Aggressive behavior*** can be loud, mean, challenging, and/or yelling. One possibility is for the leader to give the students these definitions of the words and then ask the students to be researchers during the next week and write down examples of assertive, nonassertive, and aggressive behaviors.

**Examples of Role-Plays:** Freeman and Mesenberg (1983) give a registration form for each assertiveness group with each student behaving in one of the three manners.

**Example of the Nonassertive Behavior:** Joe walks slowly and hesitantly to the counter looking down. He stands and waits for the secretary to notice him. When she does, he speaks in a whisper and says,

"You don't have any more forms for the group, do you?" (p. 69).

**Example of the Aggressive Behavior:** Shari storms to the counter looking in all directions, calls for the secretary's attention, even though she can see the secretary is on the telephone. She leans on the counter and yells, "Gimme one of those assertive registration forms right now!" (p. 69).

**Example of the Assertive Behavior:** Shawn walks up to the counter looking directly at the secretary. He smiles and waits for her to look up from her work. Using a pleasant tone of voice, he leans forward and says, "I would like a form for the assertive group please" (p. 69).

Students need to be able to analyze these examples prior to collecting their own examples during the coming week.

In a book entitled *The New Assertive Woman*, Bloom, Coburn, and Pearlman (1975) gave an assertive bill of rights. This assertive bill of rights is as follows:

1. The right to be treated with respect.

2. The right to have and express your own feelings and opinions.

3. The right to be listened to and taken seriously.

4. The right to set your own priorities.

5. The right to say no without feeling guilty.

6. The right to ask for what you want.

7. The right to get what you pay for.

8. The right to ask for information from professionals.

9. The right to make mistakes.

10. The right to choose not to assert yourself.

The group leader may wish to use this as a guide for developing the parameters of assertive behavior. An assertive inventory has been adapted for this age group (Activity 4A). The students can complete this worksheet to highlight areas in which they may want to role-play assertive situations. In the role-play the suggestion is that the group facilitators model role-playing the nonassertive and then the aggressive individual following which the student would change both of those two types of behaviors into assertive behaviors. Another possibility for a teaching technique would be to turn this situation into a game similar to charades in which other individuals in the group guessed if it was assertive, nonassertive, or aggressive.

**Activity 4A: ASSERTIVE CHECKLIST**

**Objective**

To find the situations in which assertiveness is hard and easy.

**Materials:** *Workbook*, pencil

**Procedure**

1. Ask the children to complete Item 1 in the *Workbook*.

2. Direct the children to complete Items 2 through 4 in the *Workbook*.

3. Tell them these situations will be used during role-playing in Session 5.

**Discussion**

Examine those situations which are hardest and have been circled in red. Discuss why those are hard for those who circled them. Maybe those who circled those same ones in green (easiest for them) could offer suggestions of why and how these are easy for them.

**Evaluation**

1. Determine whether or not the children understand the concept of assertion.

2. Decide whether or not the children know what situations are difficult for them.

3. Recognize the extent to which the children are able and willing to help each other in overcoming difficulties.

**Activity 4B: DEFINING ASSERTION**

**Objectives**

1. To describe that assertion is not aggression and is not shy.

2. To define assertion.

**Materials:** *Workbook*, pencil

**Procedure**

1. Lead a discussion about the fight picture.

2. Review with the children the information about assertive behavior (*Workbook*, Item 1) to make sure they understand. The book by Judy Tindall (1985) contains suggestions that could be helpful to you as leader.

3. Have them complete Items 2 and 3 in the *Workbook*.

4. Lead a discussion among group members about their answers to Items 2 and 3 in the *Workbook*.

5. Have them complete Items 6 and 7 in the *Workbook*.

6. Lead a discussion on what they perceive as assertive behavior.

7. Collect *Workbooks* and write comments before next Session.

## Discussion

Under Procedures 2, 4, and 6 have discussions.

## Evaluation

1. Determine how well they understand the different behaviors that can be seen and heard by persons who are assertive.

2. Assess the written answers as well as the discussions.

# SESSION 5

## AGGRESSIVE AND NONASSERTIVE BEHAVIORS

### Purposes of Session 5

1. To distinguish among assertive, aggressive, and nonassertive behaviors.

2. To help children become more assertive in expressing their feelings.

In this Session distinguishing among the three types of behavior—assertive, aggressive, and nonassertive—is continued. In participants *Workbook* are illustrations to help in understanding differences and activities are suggested to help learn how to be assertive.

The material presented in Leader Background is for the leader. If time permits, these concepts could be introduced and used. They could be added to existing Activities in Session 5 or to an additional Activity the leader adds.

### Background Information

The transactional analysis series by Alvin and Margaret Freed (1977) entitled *The New TA for Kids* has a chapter on what they called "TA Rackets." Essentially, one could conceive of this as a chapter on assertiveness. Essentially, the idea of **the racketeer** is someone who uses "threats, anger, or violence to force the victim to keep his feelings in and to pay him not to hurt him, break up his store, injure his family or do other mean things to him." (p. 71) Thus, the "racketeer", or gangster, is someone who covers up their true feelings while always acting angry. The "racketeer" is someone who may be aggressive or act in a way that may be mean or demanding or it is also someone who may not be nonassertive in a way that is manipulative of other people. People who use the "rackets" are not behaving assertively. The TA series gives some examples of family rackets, some of those are as follows:

You'll make me nervous if you _____.

You know when you do that I get worried.

You've done it again, now I'll be depressed all day.

Do it again and we won't go on the trip.

Don't bother me, I'll be all right.

You know I can't stand a messy kitchen. (p. 73)

The idea of the TA series is that we use these "rackets" to protect ourselves. In fact, we are protecting ourselves from our true feelings.

In a book by Canfield and Wells (1976) they described what they called **killer statements and gestures** in which they discussed the continuum of assertive, nonassertive, and aggressive behavior. Basically, the "killer" statements and gestures are aggressive forms of behavior. Canfield and Wells (1976) discussed this as follows:

> Have you ever worked very hard at something you felt was not understood or appreciated? What was it? What was said or done that made you feel your effort was not appreciated . . . ? Were you afraid that people might put you or it down? What kinds of things might they say or do that would put you, your ideas or your achievements down? (p. 67)

They gave examples of "killer" statements that are as follows:

> We don't have time for that now.
>
> That's a stupid idea - you know that's impossible.
>
> You're really weird, are you crazy, retarded, kidding me, serious.
>
> Only boys/girls do that.
>
> Wow, he's strange man, really strange.
>
> That stuff is for sissies. (p. 67)

Canfield and Wells suggested that students can make collages of "killer" statements in which they can address the question "Why do people use "killer" statements?" This would be very similar to looking at the issue of why people use aggressive behavior.

## Activity 5A: IDENTIFY AGGRESSIVE BEHAVIOR

### Objectives

1. To understand what aggressive behavior is.

2. To know what one can observe in aggressive people.

3. To know what one often will hear aggressive people say.

**Materials:** *Workbook*, pencil

### Procedure

1. Review with the children the information about aggressive behavior (*Workbook*, Item 1) to make sure they understand.

2. Have them complete Item 2 in the *Workbook*.

3. Lead a discussion among group members about what aggressive behavior is. Help them understand what can be observed and often heard as statements from these people. As much as possible, help these children to understand why the person behaves that way and how the person could gain different feelings so as to become more assertive.

4. Role-play some aggressive behaviors as suggested in *Workbook*, Item 4. You may want to do more in role-playing as suggested in introductory remarks to Session 4, Leader Manual.

5. Lead a discussion on what they learned from the role-playing.

6. Collect the *Workbook* and write Leader's Comments before the next Session.

**Discussion**

Under Procedure 3 and 5 have discussions.

**Evaluation**

1. Determine whether or not they understand differences between assertive and aggressive behaviors.

2. Ascertain whether or not they understand why aggressive people behave as they do and how or what would need to change so as to be more assertive about their feelings and less aggressive.

**Activity 5B: IDENTIFY NONASSERTIVE BEHAVIOR**

**Objectives**

1. To understand what nonassertive behavior is.

2. To know what one can observe in nonassertive people.

3. To help children understand how changing from nonassertive to assertive behavior can be beneficial in expressing their feelings.

**Materials:** *Workbook*, pencil

**Procedure**

1. Review with the children the information about nonassertive behavior (*Workbook*, Item 1) to make sure they understand.

2. Have them complete Item 2 in the *Workbook*.

3. Lead a discussion among group members about what nonassertive behavior is. Help them understand what can be observed and often heard or not heard as statements from these people. As much as possible, help these children to understand why the person behaves that way and how the person could gain different feelings so as to become more assertive.

4. Role-play some nonassertive behaviors as suggested in *Workbook*, Item 4. You may want to do more in role-playing using other situations from Activity 4A or others you or group members suggest.

5. Lead a discussion on what they learned from the role-playing.

6. Collect the *Workbook* and write Leader's Comments before the next Session.

**Discussion**

Under Procedures 3 and 5 have discussions.

**Evaluation**

1. Determine whether or not they understand differences between assertive and nonassertive behaviors.

2. Ascertain whether or not they understand why nonassertive people behave as they do and how or what would need to change so as to be more assertive about their feelings and less nonassertive.

**NOTE:** Activity 5C necessitates assignment a few days ahead of class discussion.

## Activity 5C: RESEARCH NOTES

### Objectives

1. To have group members to observe in others what they have been studying in their groups.

2. To have group members to gather from real life examples of assertive, aggressive, and nonassertive behaviors.

**Materials:** *Workbook*, pencil

### Procedure

1. A few days ahead of group discussion of this activity, assign group members to be researchers and collect examples of assertive, aggressive, and nonassertive behaviors.

2. Ask them to record their observations in the *Workbook*, Items 2, 3, and 4.

3. Lead a discussion as indicated in *Workbook*, Item 6.

4. If you believe doing so would be helpful, use more role-plays or collages to help the students understand the difference among assertive, nonassertive and aggressive behavior. For example, the leader can use the Freeman and Mesenberg (1983) role-play which was discussed in Session 4.

5. Lead a discussion on *Workbook*, Item 7.

6. Collect the *Workbook* and write Leader's Comments before the next session.

### Discussion

Under Procedures 3 and 5 have discussions.

## Evaluation

1. From reviewing their entries for *Workbook*, Items 2, 3, and 4, determine whether or not they understand differences among the three types of behaviors.

2. From their discussions determine whether or not they perceive

   a. The usefulness of assertive behaviors and

   b. The value of changing their behaviors so as to be more assertive and less nonassertive and/or less aggressive.

# SESSION 6

## ANGER

**Purpose of Session 6**

To explore anger and the appropriate expression of anger.

**Background Information**

The importance of having a unit on assertiveness prior to a unit on anger is that the group facilitator can build from the idea of the assertive expression of feelings and work with the children to find ways to assertively express their anger. An additional way to introduce the idea of anger is to make it clear that anger comes out in many ways. For example, you can refer back to the "TA rackets" and to the "killer" statements that were previously discussed. Inappropriately expressing anger violates the assertive rights of other people in that it often does not treat the individual with respect. One important note for group facilitators is that anger is an emotion with which many Americans have a difficult time dealing, so do not be surprised if you feel some discomfort as you work on this unit. Often leaders have discomfort in trying to determine what is appropriate expression of anger.

### Activity 6A: ANGRY WORKSHEET

**Objectives**

1. To understand the type of events that we associated with anger.

2. To understand that anger exists upon a continuum.

**Materials:** *Workbook*, pencil

**Procedure**

1. Direct the children to write their experiences in their *Workbooks* to complete Items 1 through 4.

2. Discuss experiences that made them angry.

3. Focus on one experience per child that made him/her angry during the past week. The leader could then have the child identify that time and then try to identify how angry it actually made them.

4. Direct children to talk about what they did to deal with their anger.

5. Ask each child to complete *Workbook*, Item 6. A group discussion may be needed to help individuals to complete Item 6.

6. Ask them to read and do Items 7 through 9.

7. Lead a discussion on *Workbook*, Items 8 and 9.

## Discussion

Under Procedures 2, 3, 4, 5, and 7 have discussions.

## Evaluation

1. Determine if children have an idea of how to deal with anger.

2. Assess whether they understand that anger exists in degrees.

## Activity 6B: MASKS

### Objectives

1. To learn that our faces can express our emotions.

2. To learn that some people hide their feelings under a mask.

**Materials:** *Workbook*, scissors, crayons, construction paper (optional), string, tape

**Procedure**

1. Direct children to the *Workbook* and have them cut out the "Anger Feeling Mask" that shows anger.

2. Have children color this mask. Direct them to be creative, use colors that are bold and angry. Explain how "tribal masks" often look fierce and that the children can make their mask fierce as well.

3. Ask them to role-play some angry situations using the mask they colored.

4. Have them discuss their feelings, what they observed in each other, and what they learned about themselves and their behaviors in anger.

5. Have them look at the second mask "Hide-A-Feeling Mask" which is worn when we are mad but are "faking it" by trying to look a different way.

6. Explain how we sometimes can fool other people with our "Hide-A-Feeling Mask" but that our true feelings remain the same.

7. Role-play some situations in which one "Hides-A-Feeling."

8. Discuss how and why we use the "Hide-A-Feeling Mask."

9. Have them discuss Items 11 and 12.

10. Collect *Workbooks* and record Leader's Comments before next Session.

**Discussion**

1. Ask children to discuss the idea of "masks."

2. Lead discussions as identified in Procedures 4, 7, and 8.

**Evaluation**

1. Determine whether or not group members understand "masks" and the way we cover our true feelings.

2. Ascertain whether or not group members gained a desire to remove their "masks" regarding feelings and more toward being more open, honest, and responsible.

**Activity 6C: FEELING WHEEL**

**Objectives**

1. To teach that many feelings are associated with anger.

2. To help children understand why feelings of anger often are accompanied by other feelings.

**Materials:** *Workbook*, pencil

**Procedure**

1. Ask children to complete individually *Workbook* Items 1 through 4.

2. Lead a discussion as group members share their "Feeling Wheels," *Workbook*, Item 5.

3. Ask each individual to complete *Workbook*, Items 6 and 7.

4. Lead a discussion based on Items 6 and 7.

5. Lead a discussion based on their responses to *Workbook*, Item 9.

6. Collect *Workbook*s and add Leader's Comments before the next meeting.

**Discussion**

Lead discussion as identified in Procedures 2, 4, and 5.

**Evaluation**

Determine if they realize that different feelings can co-exist.

# SESSION 7

# MY STRENGTHS

## Purposes of Session 7

1. To identify each child's personal strengths.

2. To help each child feel comfortable with his/her strengths.

## Background Information

The main concept in this section on personal strength is that it is possible for a person to overcome a weakness by focusing on his/her strength. The ability to recognize one's strength and to utilize one's strength is a positive coping technique, therefore, this section is intended to help children in the group understand that they do have strength and to identify it. After completing this task, the hope is that the effort will reflect positively in areas of self confidence and self image.

## Activity 7A: STAR

### Objective

To have each child value himself or herself.

**Materials:** shoe box, star, *Workbook*, pencil

### Procedure

1. Begin this activity by using a shoe box or some box with a removable or hinged lid. Have the star taped in the bottom of the box with a statement on the cover of the box that you are the most important star in the world.

2. Tell the children to keep what they see a secret as they pass the box around.

**LEADER:** Draw a star similar to the illustration or photocopy and tape star in bottom of star box.

3. As each child opens the box he/she will see a star.

4. **NOTE:** If a teacher chooses not to create the shoe box, tell a story about looking in a calm lake. Tell the children that they may see a very important person when they look in the lake. Who? They see themselves.

5. Instruct children to answers *Workbook*, Items 2 and 3.

6. Collect *Workbooks* and write Leader's Comments before the next meeting.

### Discussion

Lead a discussion on Item 3.

### Evaluation

1. Notice whether or not these children seemed happy when they looked into the box and saw a star.

2. Determine whether or not these children understand why liking one's self is essential to feeling good.

## Activity 7B: PROUD

### Objective

To have students identify something that makes them feel proud.

### Background Information

The leader can talk about feeling proud of many things. It can be something you have accomplished or something that you have achieved. The group leader should note that children who have very low self concepts will need to be prodded to complete this activity. Often times they will not find anything that makes them feel proud. At that point the group leader can ask them how they are doing in their spelling work or how they are doing in math? The leader can ask them if they have learned to swim, ride a bicycle, skateboard, climb a tree, or cook? Basically the leader will need to focus on any positive achievements made by the student.

**Materials:** *Workbook*, pencil

**Procedure**

1. Encourage children to list several accomplishments from when they were young up to the present time. Then the child should try to find an accomplishment or a source of pride from the past week.

2. Instruct children to answer Items 1 through 8 in the *Workbook*.

3. Share the sources of pride by having the children pair off and share their sources of pride, *Workbook*, Item 8.

4. Instruct partners to tell the group about the events and accomplishments that have led to pride for the individuals.

5. Collect the *Workbook*s and write Leader's Comments before the next meeting.

**Discussion**

1. Direct children to have their partner introduce them to the group. "This is _____. She or he can be proud of _____."

2. Discuss the kinds of things that make us proud.

**Evaluation**

Determine if children can select events to share as personal accomplishments.

# SESSION 8

# DECISION MAKING

## Purposes of Session 8

1. To focus on decision-making skills. The concept of decision making is an important concept to be able to teach to young children. Essentially, a major task in life is to be able to rank order your preference for activities, ways to spend your time, and later-on for job choices.

2. To help children realize what their values and ideas are.

3. To help them better understand their ideas and beliefs.

4. To formulate ideas into a statement of the problem, generate choices and alternatives in problem solving, explore long and short term consequences, and rank order their choices.

### Activity 8A: ROLE-PLAY

#### Objectives

To role-play situations in which peer pressure may influence decision making.

#### Background Information

Other programs for children have utilized decision making as a major part of their program. For example, Project CHARLIE, (5701 Normandale Road, Edina, MN 55424) uses a decision-making strategy. Project CHARLIE uses some decision making stories from Sid Simon's *Values Clarification* book (Simon, Howe, & Kirschenbaum, 1972). For example, they use Simon's story Alligator River and use a forced choice to enable the children to determine how they felt about each of the characters.

**Materials:** *Workbook*, pencils

**Procedure** (Project CHARLIE uses a role-play called "You Get the Cigarettes.")

1. Ask children to act out a situation where one child does not have a lot of friends and another child is very popular, *Workbook*, Item 1.

2. Have children to complete *Workbook*, Item 2.

3. Ask children to role-play a situation where a group of children are asking the shy child to go and buy or bring cigarettes from his/her parents store so they can all smoke.

4. Have children to complete *Workbook*, Item 4.

5. Afterward, have group members discuss the two role-plays done by the class.

6. Have the group members to discuss how peer pressure is often generated.

7. Have the group members to determine ways to resist peer pressure.

8. If time permits use other role-plays such as

   a.  deciding whether to take money from mom's purse to go buy candy.

   b.  deciding whether to leave school at noon with our friends.

9. Direct children to answer Item 8 in the *Workbook*.

10. Collect *Workbooks* for Leader's Comments.

**Discussion**

Discuss ways to resist peer pressure.

**Evaluation**

Determine if the children developed effective ways of resisting pressure.

## Activity 8B: CONTRACTS

### Objectives

1. To break decision making into small segments.

2. To develop behavioral contract where the child could set a goal for the next week and then work on developing a set of steps that would help his/her reach the goal. This way each child has both a daily activity and then a long term (one week) activity. For example:

   Long-Term Goal—To read a book.

   Daily Activity—The number of pages to be read.

3. To increase the child's self-respect as well as increase his/her "willpower."

**Materials:** *Workbook*, pencil

### Procedure

1. Instruct children to read the worksheet.

   a. The first choice is between two positive goals and the child is certain to "win" no matter which is chosen.

   b. The second is more difficult as "go out and play" is fun in the short-term. Possibly "do your homework" is beneficial more as long-term.

2. Describe that some decisions are easy and others more difficult. Indicate that both short and long-term results need to be considered.

3. Explain the "contract" as a way to set a goal and break it into separate parts so that it will be completed.

4. Lead a discussion on the contract, its parts, and its value.

5. Help each child set a goal.

6. Have each child complete the contract in Item 4 of the *Workbook.*

7. Instruct children to take "Contract" home and check off if each day's task is completed.

**Evaluation**

Determine if goals are set in small steps.

✳        ✳        ✳        ✳

# SESSION 9

## RELATIONSHIPS—FAMILY

### Purposes of Session 9

1. To help children realize the importance of relationships in their lives.

2. To emphasize the special importance of their relationship with their family and their friends.

### Activity 9A: FIND A FAMILY

#### Objective

To help children represent their family to the group.

**Materials:** *Workbook*, crayons

#### Procedure

1. Instruct children to select figures to color that will represent their family.

2. Tell children to connect their family with lines. Encourage children to make 2-families if their Mom and Dad live apart.

#### Discussion

1. Share pictures with the group.

2. Emphasize that each child's picture is different from the other pictures. Have the children note that everyone's family is unique.

#### Evaluation

Determine if children recognize differences in size and make-up of families.

## Activity 9B: FAMILY DESCRIPTION

### Objective

To describe unique aspects of their family.

**Materials:** *Workbook*, pencil

### Procedure

1. Direct children to complete *Workbook*, Items through 6.

2. Discuss what makes the family important to individuals.

### Discussion

Share similarities and differences among families.

### Evaluation

Notice whether children can accept that families can have differences.


## Activity 9C: FAMILY FAVORITES

### Objective

To illustrate families are places where each member can have favorite activities.

**Materials:** *Workbook*, crayons

### Procedure

1. Have each child draw a picture of his/her family with everyone doing something they like to do.

2. Have them share their pictures with the group.

3. Call their attention to the interaction between family members when each is doing something they enjoy.

**Discussion**

1. Instruct each child to have each family member doing a favorite family activity.

2. Discuss how a family event makes them feel special.

**Evaluation**

Notice whether children can realistically determine what other members of their family like to do.

# SESSION 10

# FRIENDSHIP

## Purposes of Session 10

1. To define qualities of a friend.

2. To find ways to be a friend.

3. To listen to music about friends (optional).

4. To end group meetings.

## Activity 10A: FRIENDSHIP

### Objectives

1. To define friendship.

2. To list ways to show friendship.

**Materials:** *Workbook*, pencil

### Procedure

1. Direct students to work in pairs or small groups.

2. Have each group fill in the worksheet.

### Discussion

1. Share findings with the whole group.

2. Ask children to share examples of a time that a friend made them feel very special.

3. Lead a discussion on Items 5 and 6.

### Evaluation

See how well they understand friendship by how many different qualities they can list.

### Activity 10B: SPECIAL PEOPLE

#### Objective

To list special people in each child's life.

**Materials:** *Workbook*, pencil

#### Procedure

1. Have each child write the names of his/her friends in the circles on the worksheet in Item 1 of the *Workbook*.

2. Tell the group that family members may be written on the friendship circle.

#### Discussion

1. Discuss with the group the qualities of each of the people listed as friends.

2. Try and find a general statement that describes a friend, *Workbook*, Items 3 and 4.

### Activity 10C: AUTOGRAPHS

#### Objective

To terminate group.

**Materials:** *Workbook*, pencil or pen

## Procedure

1. Have group members discuss what they learned from these group sessions.

2. Provide a party-like atmosphere to end group, such as treats and music.

3. Have each child to sign all *Workbooks* on Activity 10C so as to form an autograph sheet.

4. If the leader chooses, use music. Suggestions include:

    a. The "Velveteen Rabbit" by Meryl Streep and George Winston.

    b. "Glad to Have a Friend Like You" from the Marlo Thomas album "Free to be . . . you and me."

## Discussion

Discuss the importance of our feelings.

# BIBLIOGRAPHY

# BIBLIOGRAPHY

Beck, A.T. (1976). *Cognitive therapy and emotional disorders.* New York: International Universities Press.

Berscheid, E., & Walster, E. (1969). *Interpersonal attraction.* Reading, MA: Addison-Wesley Publishing.

Bloom, L.Z., Coburn, K., & Pearlman, J. (1975). *The new assertive woman.* New York: Dell.

Braswell, L., & Kendall, P.C. (1988). Cognitive behavioral methods with children. In K.S. Dobson (Ed.), *Handbook of cognitive-behavioral therapies.* New York: Guilford.

Canfield, J., & Wells, H.D. (1976). *100 ways to enhance self. Concept in the classroom: A handbook for teachers and parents.* Englewood Cliffs, NJ: Prentice-Hall.

Corey, G. (1986). *Theory and practice of counseling and psychotherapy (3rd ed.).* Belmont, CA: Brooks/Cole.

Corey, G., & Corey, M.S. (1982). *Groups: Process and prâctice (2nd ed.).* CA: Brooks/Cole.

Davis, K.E. (1985). Near and dear: Friendship and love compared. *Psychology Today, 19*(2).

Dryden, W. & Ellis, A. (1988). Rational-emotive therapy. In Dodson, K.S. (Ed.), *Handbook of cognitive behavioral therapies.* New York: Guilford.

Elkind, D. (1981). *The hurried child: Growing up too fast too soon.* Menlo Park, CA: Addison-Wesley.

Freed, A., & Freed, M. (1977). *TA for kids: Powerful techniques for developing self-esteem.* Rolling Hill Estates, CA: Jalmar Press.

Freeman, S.M., & Mesenburg, R.J. (1983). *Developing group skills: A teacher's perspective.* Developing Skills Associates (No further address or publication information available).

Glidewell, J.C., Kanter, M., Smith, L.M., & Stringer, L. (1966). Classroom socialization and social structure. In *Review of Child Development Research,* edited by M. Hoffman and L. Hoffman, pp. 221-257. New York: Russell Sage Foundation.

Ivey, A.E. (1988). *International interviewing and counseling: Facilitating client development (2nd ed.).* Belmont, CA: Brooks/Cole.

Meichenbaum, D. (1977). *Cognitive behavior modification: An integrative approach.* New York: Plenum.

Pepitone, A. (1964). *Attraction and hostility.* New York: Atherton Press.

Riley, S. (1978a). *What does it mean? Afraid.* Chicago, IL: Children's Press.

Riley, S. (1978b). *What does it mean? Angry.* Chicago, IL: Children's Press.

Riley, S. (1978c). *What does it mean? I'm Sorry.* Chicago, IL: Children's Press.

Riley, S. (1978d). *What does it mean? Sharing.* Chicago, IL: Children's Press.

Robin, A.L., Schneider, M., & Dolnick, M. (1976). The turtle technique: An extended case study of self-control in the classroom. *Psychology in the Schools, 13,* 449-453.

Rubin, Z., (1973). *Liking and loving: An invitation to social psychology.* New York: Holt, Rinehart and Winston.

Schmuck, R.A., Runkel, P., Arends, J., & Arends, R. (1977). *The second handbook of organizational development in schools.* Palo Alto, CA: Mayfield Press.

Schmuck, R.A., & Schmuck, P.A. (1979). *Group process in the classroom (3rd ed.).* Dubuque, IA: Wm. C. Brown.

Simon, S.B., Howe, L.W., & Kirschenbaum, H. (1972). *Values clarification: A handbook of practical strategies for teachers and students.* New York: Hart Publishing.

Smart, M.S., & Smart, R.C. (1978). *School-age Children: Development and relationship (2nd. ed.).* New York: Macmillan Publishing.

Steiner, C. (1977). *The original warm fuzzy tale.* Sacramento, CA: Jalmar Press.

Tester, S.R. (1979). *Sometimes I'm afraid.* Chicago, IL: Children's Press.

Tindall, J.A. (1985). *Peer power, becoming an effective peer helper: Book 1, Introductory Program.* Muncie, IN: Accelerated Development, Publishers.

Trotzer, J. (1989). *The counselor and the group: Integrating theory, training, and practice, 2nd ed.* Muncie, IN: Accelerated Development, Publishers.

Yalom, I.D. (1975). *The theory and practice of group psychotherapy (2nd ed.).* New York: Basic Books.

Zajonc, R. (1960). The concepts of balance, congruity, and dissonance. *Public Opinion Quarterly, 24,* 280-296.

# INDEX

# INDEX

## A

Acceptance Stage 17-8
Actions 6, 10
Activities for Children 3-10
Activity Titles
    4-ways to relax 70
    afraid 55-6
    afraid balloons 56-8
    anger away 63
    anger dragon 63-4
    angry worksheet 115-6
    assertive checklist 105-6
    autobiography 96-7
    autographs 84-5, 132-3
    being a friend 75-6
    brainstorm 99-100
    catch the closing 40-1
    color square 42-3
    contracts 126-7
    defining assertion 106-7
    discussion of happy and sad
      50-1
    draw a face 49-50
    draw anger 62-3
    family favorites 129-30
    family description 129
    feeling wheel 118-9
    feelings alphabet, draw a feeling
      44-5, 100
    feeling toss 101-2
    feelings tags 43-4
    find-a-family 128
    five square share 76-7
    friendship 131-2
    goodbye 83
    grab a feeling 58-9
    identify aggressive behavior
      110-1
    identify nonassertive behavior
      111-2
    intermediate group, *Figure* 91
    life line 81-2
    masks 116-8
    meet . . . me! 37-8
    music 77-8
    my favorite activity 36-7
    my mad-ometer 61-2
    name tag faces 93-4
    name tags 35-6
    new way to relax 71-3
    proud 122-3
    research notes 113-4
    role-play 124-6
    rules, rules 39-40
    share, draw, and tell 47-8
    sharing 45-6, 78-9
    silhouettes 94-5
    special people 132
    star 120-2
    T-shirt design 97-8
    too much work—too little time
      66-8
    unique you 80-1
    warm fuzzies and cold pricklies
      51-4
    worry 56
Anger 60-5, 114-9
Arends, J. 26, 76, 138
Arends, R. 26, 76, 138
Aspects
    personal 25
    professional 25
Attribution retraining 9

## B

Beck, A.T. 7, 137
Behavior
    actions 6
    aggressive 103-4, 108-11
    assertive 103-7
    nonassertive 103-4, 108-10,
      111-2
    prosocial 3
Behavior shaping 17
Beliefs
    faulty 7
    irrational 7
Bercheid, E. 74, 137
Bibliotherapy 7
Bloom, L.Z. 104, 137
Braswell, L. 8-9, 137

# C

Canfield, J. 80, 109-10, 137
Classroom
    groups 26-7
Closing Stage/Termination Stage
    19-20
Co-facilitator 14
Coburn, K. 104, 137
Cognitions 6, 10, 89
Cognitive Behavioral Therapy (CBT)
    7-9, 21
Cognitive therapy 7-8
Cognitive level 6
Cold prickly 51-4
Commitment
    group leader 25-6
Confidentiality 16
Coping 5
Corey, G. 7, 15, 25, 137
Corey, M.S. 15, 25, 137

# D

Davis, K.E. 74, 137
Decision making 124-7
    skills 5
Development
    cognitive 31
    concrete operation 31
    preoperational period 31
Discussions 19
Dobson, K.S. 137
Doinick, M. 8, 138
Dryden, W. 7, 137

# E

Elkind, D. 90, 137
Ellis, A. 7, 137
Empathy 16
Encouraging skill/technique 21-2
Essentials
    group 13-28

# F

Facilitator
    group 13-4
    role 13
Family 128-30
Feelings 6, 10, 99-102
    encouraging 17
    identify 9
    label 9, 17
    recognition 17
    sharing 42-8
    understand 9
Feelings level 6
Flexibility 31
Focusing skill/technique 22-3
Format
    each session 92
Formation
    group 23-7
Freed, A. 52, 108, 137
Freed, M. 52, 108, 137
Freeman, S.M. 103, 113, 137
Freud, S. 89
Friendship 74-9, 131-3

# G

Genuine caring 20
Gestures 109-10
Getting to know you 93-5
Glidewell, J.C. 74, 137
Group
    activities 3-10
    beginning 13
    catharsis 6
    cohesiveness 5
    development 15-20
    essentials 13-28
    facilitator 13-4
    focusing 18
    function 5-6
    norm 16
    on-task 18
    reinforcement 18
    rule 16
    size 14
    starting 23
    support 3, 5-6

Group leader
    basic skills 20-3
    commitment 25-6
    personal aspects 25
    professional aspects 25
    who can be 26
Group sessions
    activities, *Figures* 33, 91
    intermediate 90-133, *Figure* 91
    primary level 32-85, *Figure* 33
    topics, *Figures* 33, 91
Groups
    classroom 26-7
    forming 23-7
    support 15
Guidelines
    proposal 25

**H**

Happy 49-54
Homework 7, 9
Howe, L.W. 124, 138
Identification 6
Imitation 6
Importance 18
Initial stage
    tasks 16
Intervention 4-5
    short term 15
    techniques 8-9
Introduction
    meeting each other 35-8
Ivey, A.E. 10, 21, 22, 138

**K**

Kanter, M. 74, 137
Kendall, P.C. 8-9, 137
Killer statements 109, 115
Kirschenbaum, H. 124, 138
Kohlberg 89

**L**

Label 17
Leader
    responsibilities 13, 93

Leaders role
    confronting 17
    encouraging 17
Learner
    outcomes 27-8
Length of activity 33, 34, 90
Listening skill/technique 20

**M**

Manual
    grades 2 and 3 29-85
    grades 4, 5, and 6 87-133
    intermediate workbook 87-133
    primary workbook 29-85
Maslow, A. 74, 80
Meichenbaum, D. 8, 138
Modeling 6
Modeling of behavior 9

**N**

Norms
    group 16

**O**

Objective
    manual 6
Open-ended questions skill/
    technique 22
Organization 11-28
Orientation 6-10
    theoretical 6-10
Outcome
    decision making skills 28
    experience support 28
    express feelings 27-8
    learner 27-8
    make changes 28
    rely on other people 27
    take risks 28

**P**

Pearlman, J. 104, 137
Penalties 7

Pepitone, A. 74, 138
Piaget, 89
Piaget's theory 31
Positive
    enthusiasm 20
    support 20
Problem-solving training 8
Problems
    ways to resolve 18
Project CHARLIE 124, 125
Proposal
    guidelines 25

## R

Racketeer 108
Rational 3-6
Rational Emotive Therapy (RET) 7
Recognition 17
Reflecting skill/technique 20-1
Relationships—Family 128-30
Relaxation 69-73
Research
    base 7
Respect 16
Response cost 9
Responsibility Stage 18
Rewards 7, 9
Riely, S. 45, 55, 60, 138
Robin, A.L. 8, 138
Rogers, C. 80
Role-playing 9, 19
Rubin, Z. 74, 138
Rules 39-41
    group 16
Runkel, P. 26, 76, 138

## S

Sad 49-54
Schmuck, P.A. 15, 74, 138
Schmuck, R.A. 15, 26, 74, 76, 138
Schneider, M. 8, 138
Self-concept 80-5
Self-esteem 32
Self-talk 21
Session
    topics 14
Sharing 96-8

feelings 42-8
Simon, S.B. 124, 138
Skills
    See techniques
    basic 5
    group leader 20-3
Smart, M.S. 31-2, 138
Smart, R.C. 31-2, 138
Smith, L.M. 74, 137
Stage
    acceptance 17-8
    closing 19-20
    initial 15-6
    responsibility 18
    security 15-6
    termination 19-20
    work 19
Stages 15-20
Steiner, C. 52
Streep, M. 133
Strengths 120-3
Stress 4-5, 66-8
Stringer, L. 74, 137
Stroke 52
Structure 11-28
Support
    understanding sources 23,
        *Figure* 24

## T

TA Rackets 108-9, 115
Techniques 8-9
    encouraging 20
    focusing the communication 20
    group leader 20-3
    intervention 8-9
    listening 20
    open-ended questions 20
    reflecting feelings and meanings
        20
    turtle 8
Termination 14-5
Termination Stage 19-20
Tester, S.R. 55
Theoretical 6-10
Therapy 7
Thomas, M. 77, 133
Time frame 33, 34, 90

Tindall, J.A. 106, 138
Topic
    intermediate group, *Figure* 91
    primary group, *Figure* 33
Topic in Curriculum
    afraid and worried 55-9
    anger 60-5
    friendship 74-9
    happy and sad 49-54
    introduction 35-8
    relaxation 69-73
    rules 39-41
    self-concept 80-5
    sharing feelings 42-8
    stress 66-8
Topic of Curriculum
    aggressive and nonassertive
        behavior 108-14
    anger 115-9
    assertive behavior 103-7
    decision making 124-7
    feelings 99-102
    getting to know you 93-5
    my strengths 120-3
    relationships-family 128-30
    sharing 96-8
Topics
    session 14
Transfer new learning 19
Transition
    phase 89
Trotzer, J. 15, 16, 17, 18, 138
Trust
    develop 16
Turtle 8

**U**

Understanding 5

**V**

Verbal self-instructional training
    8-9

**W**

Walster, E. 74, 137

Warm-fuzzy 51-4
Welcoming 20
Wells, H.D. 80, 109-10, 137
Winston, G. 133
Work Stage 19
Workbook manual
    grades 2 and 3 29-85
    grades 4, 5, and 6 87-133
    intermediate 87-133
    primary 29-85

**Y**

Yalom, I.D. 5

**Z**

Zajonc, R. 74

# ABOUT THE AUTHOR

Photo by Steve Hermann

**Kristi Lane,** Child Psychologist and Educator, is a Professor of Psychology at Winona State University. Prior to joining the faculty of Winona State University, she worked with early intervention programs, with children displaying behavioral disturbance, and in clinical settings. Dr. Lane received her bachelor's degree in psychology from the University of North Carolina at Charlotte and her doctorate in psychology from Peabody College of Vanderbilt University. She is licensed as a School Psychologist and as a Licensed Consulting Psychologist.

Her research and applied interests have centered on preventative efforts designed to promote children's well-being and early intervention. She believes that efforts directed in these directions will bring multi-fold benefits. She is interested in the ecological psychology of the child in relation to his/her family, peers, school, community, and world. She likes to direct her efforts at assisting educators as they integrate the academic and emotive domains. She believes that teachers are primary mentoring figures for children.

Dr. Lane has presented papers at over 30 conferences. She has published numerous articles. Most recently her articles include "Feelings Group for Intermediate Age Children" and "Intervening to Reduce the Risk to Children During Change."

Her relaxation interests include bicycling, traveling, reading, and showing her dog.